Henry Robert Reynolds

Light and peace

Sermons and addresses

Henry Robert Reynolds

Light and peace

Sermons and addresses

ISBN/EAN: 9783337160227

Printed in Europe, USA, Canada, Australia, Japan

Cover: Foto ©Lupo / pixelio.de

More available books at **www.hansebooks.com**

LIGHT AND PEACE

SERMONS AND ADDRESSES

BY

HENRY ROBERT REYNOLDS, D.D.

PRINCIPAL OF CHESHUNT COLLEGE

NEW YORK
E. P. DUTTON & CO.
31, WEST TWENTY-THIRD STREET
1892

DEDICATORY PREFACE
ADDRESSED TO THE FORMER STUDENTS OF
CHESHUNT COLLEGE.

———❖———

MY DEAR FRIENDS,
   I can scarcely do other than, in the first instance commend these meditations to your generous consideration and acceptance. During several years, I was precluded by physical weakness from undertaking any service more public than a daily ministry to the religious and intellectual progress of those of you, who were preparing in this College for the ministry of the gospel in various Churches of Great Britain, and in many departments of home and foreign service.

  The majority of these discourses were prepared for our weekly meetings for devotion and addressed primarily to yourselves. It is, therefore, only under protest, with extreme diffidence, and in an indirect fashion that I can allow myself to be reckoned among "the preachers of the age."

  The prominent idea in this particular series of discourses is the recognition of the genuine relation that prevails between religious ideas and holy living.

Faith rests on conviction of truth, and is the *radix omnium virtutum*. Faith is light, and light is sometimes peace. When light flashes out of darkness for our behoof, it does not merely appeal to our admiration, but shines to point out our pilgrim way.

I have endeavoured, in Sermons I. and II., to show that the intelligent apprehension of the glory of God in the face of Jesus Christ illumines the darkest places of our thought, our duty, and our destiny. Sermons III.–XII. are variations of the same melody, and are so far related as to show that the law of the spirit of life, the laws of surrender, of growth and sacrifice, and the standard of union among Christians are derived from the best light that has been given us touching the very character and nature of God Himself. Fresh illustrations arise in following the lines of consecrated service, the necessity for combat, and the powers of love and waiting, which one by one issue in a peace that passeth all understanding.

The last sermon is the record of an address that preceded the celebration of the Holy Communion in the College Chapel, in January, 1887, when a large number of you assembled to realize afresh your brotherhood in Christ Jesus. The tokens of your friendship and affection have been rare and rich; and should the perusal of this record of a time of refreshment soothe an hour of missionary toil, or stir some pulse of pastoral duty in these great days of mingled storm and light, it will cheer the close of my prolonged and quiet ministry at Cheshunt College.

February, 1892.

CONTENTS.

THE KNOWLEDGE OF THE GLORY OF GOD.

"Seeing it is God that said, Light shall shine out of darkness, who shined in our hearts, to give the light [illumination, R.V. marg.] of the knowledge of the glory of God in the face of Jesus Christ."—2 COR. iv. 6 1

Preached at Emmanuel Church, Cambridge, November, 1891.

THE LIGHT OF THE KNOWLEDGE OF THE GLORY.

"The light [illumination, R.V. marg.] of the knowledge of the glory of God in the face of Jesus Christ."—2 COR. iv. 6 ... 19

Preached at Emmanuel Church, Cambridge, November, 1891.

THE MINISTRATION OF THE SPIRIT.

"How shall not the ministration of the Spirit be rather glorious?" —2 COR. iii. 8 33

Preached at East Parade Chapel, Leeds.

THE TENTH BEATITUDE.

"Ye ought ... to remember the words of the Lord Jesus, how He Himself said, It is more blessed to give than to receive." —Acts xx. 35 53

CONTENTS.

ST. PAUL A DEBTOR.

"I am debtor both to Greeks and to Barbarians; both to the wise and to the foolish. So, as much as in me is, I am ready to preach the gospel to you also that are in Rome."—ROM. i. 14 ... 73

Preached in Mansfield College Chapel, Oxford, Jan. 18, 1891, in aid of the work of the London Missionary Society.

THE SEED OF THE KINGDOM.

"And He said, So is the kingdom of God, as if a man should cast seed upon the earth, and should sleep and rise night and day, and the seed should spring up and grow, he knoweth not how. The earth beareth fruit of herself; first the blade, then the ear, then the full corn in the ear. But when the fruit is ripe straightway he putteth forth the sickle, because the harvest is come."—MARK iv. 26-29 ... 89

Preached in East Parade Chapel, Leeds.

THE IDEAL AND STANDARD OF CHRISTIAN UNITY.

"That they all may be one, even as Thou, Father, art in Me, and I in Thee, that they may be one in Us: that the world may believe that Thou didst send Me."—ST. JOHN xvii. 21   103

Preached in East Parade Chapel, Leeds.

THE POWERS OF HOLY LOVE.

"The greatest of these is love."—I COR. xiii. 13 ... 116

FAITH THE MEASURE OF BLESSING.

"Great is thy faith: be it done unto thee even as thou wilt."—ST. MATT. xv. 28 ... 133

Preached in Cheshunt College Chapel, June 28, 1821, at the ordination of two students appointed for missionary service.

CONTENTS. ix

THE FULNESS OF THE BLESSING OF THE CHRIST.

"When I come unto you, I shall come in the fulness of the blessing of the Christ."—ROM. xv. 29 149

Preached at Hastings, June 3, 1891, on the eve of the departure of a young missionary for foreign service.

WAITING UPON THE LORD.

"They that wait upon the Lord shall renew their strength; they shall mount up with wings as eagles; they shall run, and not be weary; they shall walk, and not faint."—ISA. xl. 31 ... 163

CONSECRATION OF HEARTS AND THINGS.

Address preceding the celebration of the Holy Communion at the opening of the Mansfield College, Oxford, October 15, 1889 181

"MINISTERS THROUGH WHOM YE BELIEVED."

Address preceding the celebration of the Holy Communion at Cheshunt College Chapel, at the formation of the Cheshunt Union of Former Students, January 16, 1888 195

THE KNOWLEDGE OF THE GLORY OF GOD.

Preached November, 1891, at Emmanuel Congregational Church, Cambridge.

THE KNOWLEDGE OF THE GLORY OF GOD.

"The knowledge of the glory of God in the face of Jesus Christ."—
2 COR. iv. 6.

ONLY a few of the sons of men enjoyed the strange and wonderful experience of gazing into the face of Jesus Christ. Only a few hints are given to us of what they saw and felt when they did so. A group of His earliest disciples saw His glory, and under that spell said very startling things. One exclaimed, "Thou art the Christ," and another, "Thou art the Son of God." The mighty Baptist found in Him one mightier than himself, and in strange prophetic trance cried, "Behold the Lamb of God." Peter wailed in agony, "Depart from me, I am a sinful man." The Samaritan looked into that face and exclaimed, "I perceive that Thou art a prophet." The leper prayed, "Lord, if Thou wilt, Thou canst make me clean." The officers said to the Sanhedrin, "Never man spake like this Man." A ruler of the Jews gazed into His face, and said, "We know that thou art sent from God." A Roman centurion exclaimed, "Truly this man was the Son of God." When His treacherous disciple caught sight of His face in the dark night of the betrayal, "he went out and wept bitterly."

Every human face is a mask through which streams the light of an otherwise invisible reality. Every face is moreover covered with a mysterious script which others imperfectly strive to interpret; each face conceals, and yet partially reveals, a history. The dimples of childhood and the wrinkles of age alike proclaim their complexity and mystery. The character, the temperament, the past and the future of every life are depicted on the face. The effort to repress expression has its own cipher. Even our purpose to hide our emotion involuntarily proclaims itself upon the mystic veil that we draw over our inner and real self. We often interchange the word "face" with the other terms by which we denote individuality. Art has represented for us its idea of our greatest men, but such portraiture is only a faint approximation to the reality. "The exterior semblance belies the soul's immensity." And if this be true of a little child "whose fancies from afar are brought," how much more is it true of the face of Jesus Christ! Every effort hitherto made to conceive or pourtray this face, by line or hue or word, has been a failure from the nature of the case. Painting and poetry have perhaps succeeded best when they have sought to represent the Child Jesus, or the dead Christ. This is because in the effort to do the impossible, artists have been able in these regions to utilize two proximate reserves of power. With the ideal Child, they have been able to draw upon the resources or characteristics of ripened years, so that the Infant has seemed more than an infant by some faint touch of the Ancient of days. So, in depicting the corpse of the Crucified, the painter has been able to draw upon the resources of life, and to make death pulsate with some strange hints of a victory over itself.

But while Raphael and Tintoret, Dürer and Francia

have expounded to us with some satisfaction the infant or the dead Christ, yet Raphael and Da Vinci and every modern master of form and colour have failed to set forth even their own imagination of the *man* Christ. Colours, lines, and words are equally powerless to do more than hint at absolute perfection. The face which troubled the Sanhedrin and confounded Roman power and hushed the maddened prejudice of a reckless and murderous mob,—the face to which little children turned with confiding love, and before which penitent harlots and the dying brigand found the uttermost consolation, transcends representation. The face which was set against all evil, and whose glance unmasked hypocrisy and broke the hearts of treacherous disciples,—which read all that was in man, and saw into the depths of heaven, —which at times shone above the brightness of the sun, and lavished the sense of an infinite benediction upon the helpless and unworthy, presents an impossible problem to the artist, the poet, or the man of science. The historian, whether scientific or picturesque, offers us sometimes an unintelligible and sometimes a monstrous combination which has no verisimilitude or realism, and which criticism readily consumes in its crucible.

If we can trust the only authorities we possess, we have to see, with the eyes of imagination and faith, One in our own nature, image, and likeness, who, nevertheless, repeatedly claimed to hold the destinies of all men and generations in His hand. We are called upon to believe that there did once enter into the life of our race a Personage whom born Jews believed to be more royal than David, wiser than Solomon, greater than the prophets, mightier than Moses or Elias, more august than their temple, more holy than their Sabbath. How can pen, or pencil, or word set forth a face which revealed at one and the same time the uttermost self-abandonment and the highest self-consciousness; which was the expression of the loftiest moral ideal, and yet without a trace or quiver of conscious sin, or even demerit? How can we pretend fully to realize a human life which was meek and gentle, and yet capable of delivering the most terrible judgments upon every form of selfishness, hypocrisy, and sin; which, while the embodiment of the deepest humility, yet did not hesitate to claim equality with God, a oneness with the Father and a consciousness of being, even while He spake to men, *in heaven?* We trace to some extent the lonely path of the Son of Man till we find Him the object of the concentrated hatred of His contemporaries, the victim of every passion and lie which was disgracing humanity. But how can we realize that face, the very breath of whose mouth might have consumed His enemies and blasted His executioners, but which yet turned in infinite compassion upon His bloodthirsty foes, fulfilled a sublime purpose in submitting to the shame and curse of sin, and gave Himself up, demonstrating thereby the condemnation of all sin, and the terms of Divine suffering on which alone the Eternal Righteousness could and did pardon it? We have to think of One who died and rose again in the human form which had been humbled to the death of the Cross, and so conferred upon it a glory which abolished death. We have to realize a human life and death which brought into the consciousness of those who witnessed it "the Lamb slain from the foundation of the world," and opened such a door in heaven, that our faith can even now see that He is "the Lamb of God in the midst of the throne." When those who perpetrated the most tragic deed of all time discovered what they had done, they shrieked with fear, until they saw, through the coming judgment and on the cloud of doom, the bow of promise, and the mystery of infinite love. When St. Paul caught sight of this stupendous fact, that the Christ, whom his contemporaries had crucified and whose followers he had himself madly persecuted, was "the Lord of Glory" and the Christ of all the prophetic hopes of his people, his life was transfigured and revolutionized. He was eager to confess that he counted "all things but loss for the excellency of the knowledge of Christ Jesus." Now, St. Paul here speaks of the face, the visible presentment of this mysterious Personality.

What consideration can aid our endeavour to think out for ourselves this astounding paradox? What hypothesis suggests the only satisfactory interpretation of this transcendent manhood? Who can tell us what it means to us?

The difference between the other great men of the human race and the personality of the Christ is so vast as to be immeasurable. The face of Buddha or Zerdusht, of Confucius or Mohammed, the face of Socrates, Aurelius, Francis, or Loyola may demand long and careful meditation, but we can take the parallax of these men. Moses and St. Paul himself present grand themes for the historic imagination, but they do not confound our sense of proportion. We are not intensely anxious to learn their judgment upon our character or destiny. But a restless yearning arises to know what Jesus thinks of us, and to discover some worthy explanation of the personality of the Son of Man. We are resolved, as every generation before ours has resolved, that if it be possible we will find out what the Christ is, what the Christ thinks of our life, and what actual personal relation we sustain to Him.

The various solutions that have been hazarded of this

amazing problem make our hearts throb. Our own generation is especially rife with suggestions. The very air of this nineteenth century is as full of them as was that of the second century. The Gnostic and Oriental philosophy, Alexandrine metaphysics, mediæval scholasticism, Western science, the speculations of Newtonians and Darwinians have one after the other been absorbed with the transcendent theme. No age can afford to ignore a series of facts which has effected an undeniable revolution in every department of life and thought and action.

We do not affect to deny that one tendency of human thought, from the first century to our own day, has ignored the difficulty of the problem, nor that many have said Jesus was the production of His own age; that He was the evolution of a consummate flower upon the barren stock of humanity. To many, He was simply Judaism or Rabbinism at its best. Others add that Hellenic wisdom or Oriental exaggeration touched the memory of Jesus with a mythical lustre. It is supposed by some that the law of evolution will account for the entire manifestation, and for all the history of the subsequent influence of the strange meteoric flash of His passing across the stage of this world.

Much that was once thought of as sporadic or supernatural has undoubtedly been shown to be the natural outcome of previous circumstances. Yet there are more mysteries for us to-day in the stellar heavens than either Newton or Laplace dreamed of. These multiply with every fresh organ or triumph of research. The passage from nothing to something still confounds the disciple of pre-organic evolution. The advent of life upon the planet, and the distance between the highest vertebrate and man, provoke the most urgent inquiry. And I suppose that even the theistic evolution of *history* will long be troubled with a few facts in the development of Christianity. *E.g.*, no critics hesitate to admit that Saul the persecutor wrote these weighty words, addressing them to a European community within thirty years of the death upon the cross of Jesus of Nazareth. That bare historic fact speaks volumes. In itself, it seems to me to be as startling as any supernatural event reported in Holy Scripture.

These words suggest, however, the hypothesis which satisfied St. Paul's own mind. Nearly nineteen centuries of infinitely varied experience have verified the intuition. The supposition was this, that the GLORY OF GOD was visible IN THE FACE OF JESUS CHRIST. All who are imperatively summoned to say what they think of Christ, come more or less to an identical conclusion.

St. Paul's illustration is very remarkable. He fastened upon what he believed, and what we in this year of grace also believe, to have been the primal act of Divine energy, or creative might and wisdom, when "light" broke on the universal darkness. The apostle took his stand beside the author of Genesis. He saw in "Holy Light . . . since God is Light . . . Bright effluence of Bright Essence Increate." No lower conception, no less imposing parallel satisfied him. He boldly declared that such a glory of God beamed from the face, and could alone interpret the personality of Jesus.

St. Paul comforted and warned the Corinthians by assuming that they with him had discovered in the face of Christ, power and purpose, character and claim answering to their loftiest ideal of what is to be worshipped and glorified. An abashed sense of irresistible power dazzled and overwhelmed him. The awful purity of the eternal essence radiated from the human life and death of Jesus, and smote him with an idea of righteousness more intense than any formal law or moral principle. The capacity of Christ to meet all the needs and peril of all men enchanted him. The manifestation of an appalling and bewildering self-sacrifice entranced and captivated him, bought him over to a life-long service. The words of the Lord Jesus, though fashioned into human speech, embraced infinitely varied suggestions, condensing the highest moral wisdom, transcending the resources of the schools, and seeming to be not the wisdom only, but the very word of the living God. This wisdom, though on its human side and in its human form limited, yet connoted an inward basis which was possessed of all the characteristics of infinity. More than this, the love of Christ was nothing short of the love of God, and it constrained him. Through Christ, Paul felt that he got right up to God Himself. This love wrought upon his heart with all the sweetness of human affection, of surpassing gentleness, of healing and forgiving grace and benign sympathy, yet, so far as he, Paul, was concerned, it dealt directly with the moral conscience, and appealed to the God-consciousness.

St. Paul was acquainted with Oriental incarnations, which overpowered and demolished the human shrines in which they were supposed to dwell; but here was the glory of the Infinite God flashing in the face of One who had lived and died and risen again among men. Western apotheoses were common enough in the views of Roman centurions or Greek sophists, but they only broke up the very idea of God into a rabble of Deities. If Græco-Roman fashion called a philosopher, a physician, a court favourite, an imperial Augustus "God," the process merely degraded and silenced the conscience, bandied profane compliments, and lowered the very conception of God Himself into a blasphemous superlative for the use of the market, the camp, or the schools; but *here, in the face of Jesus Christ*, was a conception which was more than all the legendary incarnations, more than all the political deifications current in St. Paul's day. He who first commanded light to shine out of darkness, *i.e.* the absolute Eternal God, had caused His own *glory* to shine from the face of Jesus Christ, on a darkness deeper than primæval chaos. This brings to us the central word of this remarkable sentence.

St. Paul does not say that the glory of God in the face of Jesus Christ has illumined the world. His position is that the Eternal, "who commanded light to shine out of darkness, has shined in our hearts, to give the illumination of the *knowledge* of the glory of God in the face of Jesus Christ." We have therefore two themes—(1) the knowledge of the glory; (2) the light or illumination beaming forth from such knowledge.

The heavens declared the glory of God during untold millenniums; but, so far as man is concerned, the world waited for the eyes which could see it and the lips which could speak of it to their fellows.

Truth is the realization by men of fact. The fact of the glory of God must be realized as a thought by some human minds before it can become the light of all our seeing.

Granted that the deepest essence of God, the highest revelation of His nature gleamed from the dying face of Jesus, still the eye of faith and love must catch sight of the glory, transform it into thought and word, before it can illumine the darkness of human destiny. Revelation here follows all the law of Divine education of the race. God has taught mankind by the great divisions of the human family. These, again, have been illumined by the special vision and intuition of a few elect souls, who have seen into the mysteries of nature, into the depths of the heart, into the meaning of history, and clothed their thoughts in words. They have believed, and they have spoken. Their words have been light, and bread of life, and water of life to their brethren. Thanks be to God! Human eyes have perceived, human hearts have conceived, human lips have told what they saw of the glory of the Only Begotten of the Father. They absorbed the glory; they have been changed into the same image from glory to glory. They have, by their knowledge of the glory, become lights in the world.

The knowledge of the glory is indispensable to us all. The almost intolerable magnificence of the sky is lavished upon us by day and night from generation to generation; yet how few form the faintest conception of its meaning. Nature is a sealed book to the enormous majority of the human family, who pass across its stage and neither see nor know. So God's unveiling of Himself in Christ falls often upon eyes that are veiled and blinded and do not see nor know. The prophetic hope of the Church is that a day is coming when no one shall have need to "say to his brother, 'Know the Lord,' for all shall know Him," and "the knowledge of the Lord shall cover the earth." Every eye shall be opened, and shall see Him before long. Meanwhile, the most urgent work of the Church is to open men's eyes, and to compel old and young, wise and unwise, to see this great glory, to look and live.

Verily no one set form of words can do more than make a faint approximation to all the reality; yet all theology consists of efforts to put into form the supreme fact of the glory of God in the face of Jesus Christ.

This has been by no means an easy task. Other thoughts and other knowledge have threatened this new thought with annihilation. Thus, *e.g.*, in grasping this supreme and illuminating fact of the incarnation of God in Christ, men have had to encounter two positions which were more fundamental still—the unity of God and the perfect humanity of Jesus. Neither of these truths could be surrendered. The *first* is the most certain dictum of the moral conscience, and of the highest philosophy, and is the grandest tradition of our race: and the second is the stupendous fact, the quality of which has given rise to the overwhelming conviction of the early believers, that God was in Christ, and the Word was made flesh in Him. Yet it must be conceded that the vast conception, that "the Word was made flesh" in Christ, and that "He took up His tabernacle" with men, and that they "beheld His glory," and saw that it was "the glory of the only begotten Son of God, a fulness of grace and truth," somewhat confounded and imperilled their faith in the Divine Unity, and in the perfect humanity of the Lord Jesus. Sometimes they expressed themselves so loosely that their enemies charged them with hero-worship akin to that which they were summoning an idolatrous world to relinquish. Their answer was that the glory of God was effulgently beaming in the face of Jesus Christ. Then the reply was that they must be splitting up their idea of God into that of two or more Gods of different degrees and faculties. This charge was vehemently repelled by those who knew that the unity of God was the prime anchor of their faith and their morals, the only safeguard against a widespread dualism, and a reality for the confession of which they were ready to sacrifice life.

Yet in repudiating a mere hero-worship, on the one hand, or any form of polytheism on the other, the early believers refused to blend the human and Divine in their thought of Christ, into a *tertium quid*, that was neither Divine nor human—not human enough to understand our experience, nor Divine enough to create and save.

What, then, was the problem which was set before them? They found, in their effort to *know* the glory of God in the face of Jesus Christ, that they must simply state all the facts that were indubitable to them. The speculative puzzles and theories were one by one laid aside, and they boldly resolved to take their stand on the facts without solving the mystery.

This kind of "knowledge of the glory of God" is not unlike the knowledge of the facts of gravitation. The generalization, in which modern philosophy rests calmly, does not expound the mystery nor explain the nature of the force which accounts for the falling of a leaf and the shape of a tear, for the swing of the pendulum and the motions of the satellites, but it states the operation of one great and universal law of the relations of matter to itself. In like manner the Christian consciousness finds, without solving the mystery of the relation of the Infinite and Finite, that it does not dare to relinquish any of the facts of this sublime synthesis, and strives to express them all—the unity of the Godhead, the humanity of Jesus, the Divinity of the Christ, the knowledge of the glory of God in the face of Jesus the Christ.

Doubtless, there are still and always have been those who, while accepting some one or more of these factors, disregard the rest. Thus, at the present moment, there are many lofty spirits who so far deviate from this knowledge that they are content with the sublime ideal of character, of self-sacrifice, of humanity which Jesus has left as His legacy to the world. They accept some of His teaching concerning both God and man. They rightly believe it to be the most lofty and veracious which has been uttered in this world, and they even transfer to the world's idea of "the Father," thoughts which are only possible to the Church as inferences derived from the incarnation of God in Him. The Christ is thus impoverished by them, and the idea of the Father is built up of unproved *ipse-dixits*, against which our modern science of nature and our ethical pessimism easily prevail. The light of the knowledge of Jesus, as He was eighteen hundred years ago, is certainly brighter than the light of the knowledge of Buddha, of Socrates, or of Marcus Aurelius; but if it be of the same character or kind, it leaves us always at liberty to repudiate it, or search for what is better. The humanity alone is insufficient to explain the history of the knowledge of the glory of God in the face of Jesus Christ. The Eternal has drawn near men in that wondrous Personality. Their destiny is proclaimed by those loving lips. Heaven blazes forth upon them in that face. His word is eternal truth. Their knowledge is to them the Eternal Life itself. Because they know that He lives, they live also.

But, on the other hand, there are those—and they have been far more numerous—who have so dwelt upon the Divine element in the Christ, have so sunned themselves in the glory of God in the face of Jesus Christ, that Jesus, the Saviour, the Brother, the sympathizing Friend, the one

Mediator between God and man, has been practically ignored. One issue has been that they have reincarnated His Godhead in that of His virgin mother. We glorify God in the mighty function ascribed to this vessel of grace, and declare, with angels and saints, that she is "blessed among women;" but the very cause and glory of God in the incarnation seem pitilessly shorn of their lustre by lifting another into the place which the Divine Son has never deserted. If, by filling our eyes with the Deity of His Person, we virtually lose thus the true humanity of Jesus, we sacrifice one prime factor in our knowledge of the glory of God in the face of Jesus Christ. He is all and infinitely more to us than we have any reason for believing that she or any other of His saints can be.

Again, if we forego our hold on the union between the Man Christ Jesus and the Eternal Son of God, our ideas of both have a strange propensity to part asunder, and we are practically, as well as theoretically, left to a mere humanity of Christ on the one side, and to an inaccessible Deity on the other. The knowledge of the glory of God in the face of Jesus Christ,—such "knowledge," indeed, as in our weakness and helplessness we can frame—becomes a compendium of the entire revelation of God. The excellency of it transcends that of all other knowledge. In it we realize facts about God and man, about perfection and corruption, about sin and redemption, about eternity and time, and about the blending of the two, about the possibilities of life and the real significance of death, which surpass all other facts, all other teaching. We grasp them in their simplest form by pondering the life of Jesus, by waiting near His cross, and by the powers of holy responsive love. A little child can accept the revelation. "Even so, Father, for thus it seemed good in Thy sight!" Often concealed from wise and prudent ones, it is unveiled to babes. The longest human life, the most intense religious experience, avails to fill up a portion only of the outline which is given at once to childlike faith; and the noblest of the apostles, at the close of his martyrlike ministry, counted all things but loss that he might know Him.

The knowledge of the glory of God in the face of Jesus Christ can only be faintly expressed in any form of words. Neither logic nor poetry, neither history nor theology, can express the fulness of this vast perception. Our worship, our sacraments, our self-sacrifice in the greatest cause, our Church life, are only the steps, the instruments by which this wisdom of the truly wise is ever growing to maturity. Our wanderings and perils, our failures and fears, reveal the heart and the power of the Shepherd of souls. The sins which we have committed, the new vistas into the universe and into eternity which open day by day, the novel enterprises to which we are called, all find encouragement or caution in this vast conception, one which brings God Himself, in all His holiness and His gentleness, in all His majesty and His mercy, so awfully, so tenderly near to our hearts.

THE LIGHT OF THE KNOWLEDGE OF THE GLORY OF GOD.

Preached in November, 1891, at Emmanuel Congregational Church, Cambridge.

THE LIGHT OF THE KNOWLEDGE OF THE GLORY OF GOD.

> " The light [the illumination] of the knowledge of the glory of God in the face of Jesus Christ."—2 COR. iv. 6.

"THE entrance of Thy word giveth light." The transformation into thought, of the blended glory and sympathy, the interwoven majesty and tenderness, of the Christ has created a new dawn in the mid-day of nature.

The light brighter than the sun which broke over the consciousness of St. Paul on his way to Damascus illumined every truth which he had already made his own. It reversed for him the highest wisdom of the past, and cancelled his inheritance in the privileges and pride of centuries. The knowledge of the glory of God in the face of Jesus Christ became so brilliant an illumination, threw such floods of light on deep problems, on obscure and unsuspected places of thought and of human experience, that he found himself in a new world, with new ideas of all things in heaven and earth, in time and eternity.

St. Paul was not alone in this matter. Every mind that has so far followed the apostle as to *know* God in *Christ*, has gone through a like experience. The effect of the glare of light which thus illumines life differs with us all in accordance with our previous circumstances. The more than meteoric splendour which breaks upon some minds in the advent of knowledge touching this supreme fact in the history of the world has in some periods so stimulated the understanding of mankind that those who saw it could do little else than try and formulate it, or endeavour to reduce the sublime synthesis to some form of creed. During hundreds of years, men could not rest in the light. It waked them so completely from their dreams, that it might seem they had forgotten the power of the light itself in their restless efforts to fit it into their previous scheme of the universe. This was not all the truth, however. New light meant new life. New life meant a strange power, and a peace which passed understanding. So that, while the philosophers and the councils were fighting about the way in which they could adequately express the relation of the Father and Son, and the relation of Jesus to both, hundreds, thousands were content to die for their Lord, and were bravely defying all the power of Roman courts, all the refinements of heathen malice, and all the cruelty of murderous mobs. They were following the Lamb whithersoever He led them, to prison and to death, and triumphing over both with songs of deliverance.

Sometimes the very same men who were most active in the intellectual endeavour to analyze the light, were also able to bear with sublime and saintly patience the uttermost cruelty of pagan hatred, and the desperate outbreaks of partisan intolerance. So through all the centuries, theological intensity has not always strangled, but rather stimulated, moral heroism and missionary enterprise.

Some special epochs have been sharply characterized by the endeavour to criticize and refine theological forms; and others, again, by the tendency to ignore the intellectual side of Christianity, and even to abandon great truths for ethical enthusiasm, or for altruistic or ascetic devotion. Every generation has its own main feature, and perhaps the most dominant sign of these times is a revolt against theology, and an unwillingness to trace the connection between the truth and the life. Surely, my brethren, this light, this illumination of the knowledge of the glory of God in the face of the Christ, is not to be simply gazed at with sharpened eyes of scientific or metaphysic subtlety, but it is to be lived by; and we have not merely to look, but to live.

Any attempt to exhaust such a theme is futile, but it may help some of you to higher life and deeper peace, if we dwell on a few of the spheres of human thought and experience upon which the glory of this light falls.

1. It illumines all the facts and laws of nature. The cross of Christ provides a new observatory of the universe. The heavens have a new meaning to us, for, if Christ be what He says that He is, He is more and greater than they; and the death of the Son of God means more to us than if we saw the whole constellation of Orion, with all its suns and nebulæ, blotted from the skies.

We, like our brethren in ancient times in the far East, who brooded over the vastness of the universe, and shrank abashed from the measureless extent of time and space, until they lost themselves, and felt that they were but helpless waves passing over the bosom of a boundless sea,—we, like them, have sometimes extinguished our sense of responsibility, and have drugged ourselves to silence and repose, while insatiable desires have been, vulture-like, gnawing at our heart. The vastness of things, the majestic sweep and awful persistence of force, the interminable and unconquerable millenniums of continuous activity have confounded and oppressed us, as they did our fathers. Neither they nor we have been able to bear these things.

Do we not turn from these considerations, as our eyes do from the unveiled disk of the sun at noon? Are we not, with our sense of the infinity of being, often baffled and crushed into helplessness and recklessness? Do we not seem veritably poised on the verge of bottomless precipices, with our sensibility quickened to morbid intensity, asking day by day, and sometimes moment by moment, "O Infinite All in One, what am I? whence have I come? whither am I going? and how can I bear to plunge me into this fathomless abyss for an eternal æon of æons without some answers to these queries, without some voice to soothe my breaking heart?"

Philosophy has often tried to answer such throbbing questions by dogmatically forcing upon us the sacrifice of self altogether, or by the endeavour to do that impossible thing—think our ego out of all existence. Again, ingenious speculations, like Pascal's or Chalmers', have bidden us find rest in the revelations of the infinitely little, where the grace and power of the Creator is also manifested, world within world, atomy within atomy, for ever. To some minds this *is* a cold bath of refreshment, but to the majority of us it gives but momentary relief. We do find, indeed, that in little things, in invisible points, in infinitesimal vibrations, the great things of the universe are effected, and in the tiniest spheres the mightiest forces of the infinite, unknowable reality are perpetually working. But oh, the enchantment of this discovery becomes a new agony! There is to these thoughts, when once we are in their clutch, no relief either from science, or common sense, or from manly fortitude, from either robust conscience or old-world maxims, from the tyranny of modern phrase or forward movements, or any other idol of the *forum;* but surely even we may rise above them and fairly grapple with them if once we realize that the Word of God has been made flesh, if it be a fact that the Eternal Life has been manifested and given to us in the Son of God. If we have come to *know* the glory of God in the face of Jesus Christ, we have in Him verily come to the centre of infinite space and eternal time. This high conception has transmuted our sense of terror into one of comparative repose. The highest light has produced the deepest peace. If the most august perfections and powers and all the glory of God flash upon us in the smile of Jesus, we cry from the depths of our heart, "My Lord and my God!" He who dwelt for ever in the bosom of God is absolutely one with Him who took the children in His arms, and hushed the storm and snatched the crown of hell and broke the spell of death. "Thanks be to God who giveth us the victory through the Lord Jesus Christ!" This is one part of the illumination; and one secret of the work of Christ is to familiarize us with the eternity to which we belong, to lead us by our union to Him up to the prime centre of it all.

2. The knowledge of the glory of God in the face of Christ illumines and enlarges and deepens our idea of God.

The least sympathetic thinkers are ready to admit, that the best and most restful concepts of Deity were originated by Jesus. But we go far beyond this, for if we know that the human personality of Jesus Christ is the best and the truest revelation of the Father, the torment and unrest of a hundred generations are absolutely stilled. We discern not only the image of God in the human heart and will, but the surest revelation of God in the highest type of man. In the knowledge of the glory of God in Christ, the Almighty comes forth from the cloud and darkness in which our feebleness of vision has enwrapped Him, and comes close to us. We know Him and are known of Him. Direct intercourse with Him becomes feasible, and the inaccessible light shines with gentle lustre on our mysterious pathway. The cry, "Father forgive them," is the whisper of the eternal love. The summons, "Come unto Me," is a voice from the excellent glory. The shout, "It is finished," rends the veil of the eternal temple from the top to the bottom. By believing in Him, we find ourselves in the holy place, in the Father's house, in the mansions prepared for us from before the foundation of the world.

3. But the illumination of this knowledge gives a new meaning to the whole of human life. Herein and hereby, we see the highest possibilities of man. Human nature is redeemed by its Head, and all the ways and types of our humanity are strangely changed by the realization of Divine glory in the ideal of it. Truth itself about God and man is transfigured. Justice is seen melting into love. All beauty, all virtue, all that is praiseworthy, all that is urged upon us by the imperative of conscience is read off afresh. We take new inspirations to our study of nature, and new motives to every act of our life. Beholding as in a mirror of perfect adequacy the glory of the Lord, we are changed into the same image from glory to glory; we drink of the river of the pleasures of God and we are satisfied.

4. Further, while such a revelation of what man may become and ought to be makes evident to us the difference

between what is possible and what is actual, we obtain the most terrible disclosure of the nature of sin, and the only light which makes it tolerable. Our first religious ideas have often proved to be a sense of conflict with God. The conviction haunts us that we have broken with the Almighty; that we have forfeited all hold upon Divine protection; that we have wilfully entangled ourselves in the consequences of broken law; that we have incurred the issues, which no obedience, no penitence, no sacrifice of ours can remit or remove. The sense of evil, of increased severance from God, and the sense of coming doom are forced upon us by conscience and by the sense of desert.

Numerous and strenuous efforts have been made by our fathers and brethren in many ages and generations to put themselves right with God. These futile endeavours have constituted the pathetic story of the world and of the religious life.

Moreover, the prince of this world boldly offers us his favour and solace, such as they are. Many voices round about us are minimizing our fault, and promising to exculpate our guilt and exonerate the transgressor. Numerous duties, innocent amusements, and necessary business do for a while distract attention from the fact. Agnostic utterances will sometimes obliterate the appalling sense of sin, and pride will whisper that we, after all, are not as other men: and yet the guilty conscience is not appeased.

There are those, on the other hand, who confidently assure our trembling spirits that *they* can pardon our offences, or guarantee our future. But though the morbid growth of self-complacency or the promises of the priest may for a while produce a seeming peace, neither knife nor anodyne stay the progress of the disease. The sins of youth or of later days hunt down or come up with the transgressor. The palliations of pride, of courage, of deceit, cease to console, the distractions of life fail to divert contemplation. The bowl is broken at the fountain of pleasure, and fear, like an armed avenger, confronts the naked soul.

But, my brethren, when we see the glory of God as the true and only solution of the face of Jesus Christ, even when He agonizes on the cross, we find then that a new light has shone upon the fiery filthy wound of our nature. This light is infinitely piercing and infinitely sympathetic. We do not cease or lose our wrath against sin—God forbid! —nor do we minimize its blame. We find it has slain *Him* and we enter into God's wrath against our sin. In our self-despair we find His unmerited pardon. We vanquish our fear because the pardon which He speaks is the principle of a new life. Our sins are not covered up; they are more conspicuous than ever in the blaze of the glory of God which radiates from the face of Jesus Christ, but, since they are the enemies and crucifiers of our dearest Friend, they are renounced. The new knowledge is a light which reveals emancipation from the curse, because we know that in our pardon an infinite expression has been given to the wrath of God against sin.

Nor need we ask any theologian, or any priest, or any philosopher to tell us *how much* of virtue, or obedience, or self-denial, or aversion to sin is necessary, nor how many prayers or Communions we should make, nor how many acts of kindness we should perform, nor how many propositions we should assent to. We eat the flesh and drink the blood of the Son of God; we dare, poor sinners that we are, to smile through our tears, because the light of the knowledge of an infinite righteousness and of an eternal love is perfect peace.

5. The light of this knowledge falls on the otherwise insoluble mystery of sorrow. I will not try to establish this mystery, or pourtray the dark shadow, or weigh the burden of life. We all know it by bitter loss and pain. Still, there are many ways in which men seek explanation of it or deliverance from it. Rivals to Christ as the great Consolator loudly proclaim their own potency. Some are persuading us to absorb ourselves with duties, and forget our sorrows. Pleasures and niceties and novelties are suggested. We are bidden to conquer the pain of bereavement by a new diversion. We are told to make a manly conquest of a morbid emotion, and that Time will dull the edge of our grief. Well, the great world is partially successful; but when we come into the light of this knowledge of the God-Man, a new meaning is given to our sorrow and to all sorrow. The wide-spread incidence of human grief may silence our wail, as in the Buddhist legend, but it will not touch the secret of our agony.[1] But, once we permit this light to shine upon our darkness, we find ourselves called into the fellowship of the Son of God, and we are reconciled.

A myriad of hearts broken beyond all human mending or time-healing have come into the fellowship of the sufferings of Christ, have taken up His cross, to bear it after Him, and they have sung in the valley of their humiliation—

"Thy way, not mine, O Lord,
However dark it be!"

[1] "What medicine is there," a bereaved mother asked of Gautama, "for my dead child?" "I know of some. I require," said he, "a handful of mustard-seed taken from a house where no son, husband, parent, or slave, has died." Thus she learned that "the living are few but the dead are many."—"Buddhaghosa's Parables," p. 108. Translated from Burmese by Captain Rogers.

and so the sorrow of the bitterest humiliation, the torture of severest pain, the threat of despair, and all the spectres of doubt have vanished like dreams of the night when morning breaks. My brethren, will you not allow this supreme truth to shine into your heart? and, if you feel the mighty secret, will you not take up the failing chorus, and proclaim to others the magic of the solace that it gives?

6. The heaviest mystery of all pain is *the silence of our dead.* No trouble is so great, so deep as this. When the veil falls we have had our last word with them, and we cannot be certain that our wildest lament pierces the shadow and the darkness which conceal our loved ones. Look at the history of the struggle with death, written in the Egyptian and Etruscan tombs, told in the most splendid of Grecian myths and of classic poetry. One can find nowhere a clear proof of reconciliation with this mystery, nor of any satisfaction with the inevitable doom, till the light of the glory of God in the face of Christ has abolished death and brought life and immortality into full view. He who holds in His hands the keys of death and of hell, says in words that have broken the silence of death, "Be thou faithful unto death, and I will give to thee the crown of life." Our dead are with Christ and He is with us.

So, my brethren, let this light shine into your hearts, and it will soothe your trembling anxieties over the awful problem of the infinite; it will reveal to you the nature of God and the possibilities of man; it will blend with your deepest sense of sin and of guilt the assurance of a full and free forgiveness; it will unriddle the mystery of pain and sorrow, of even Divine forsaking and intolerable loss, and will comfort you in the cold shadows of the tomb. But more than all, it supplies you with an ideal of duty, a motive for service, a prediction of triumph, and the only valid guide in the tremendous task now set before all Christian men and Churches, in their endeavour to heal the wounds, to wipe away the tears, and to rectify the wrongs of the world.

When this light shines upon us, we have a message to the world of heathenism, and to the nations that are groping in darkness; we have in the brotherhood of our Lord a commission which will go straight to the evils that are festering in the heart of our modern civilization. We have what we know to be the abundant justification of the existence and mission of the Church. We are certain that we have in it a remedy for all sin, all guilt, all conflict with Providence, and war between man and man. We have the open secret and the abiding possession of a peace that passeth all understanding.

THE MINISTRATION OF THE SPIRIT.

Preached at East Parade Chapel, Leeds.

THE MINISTRATION OF THE SPIRIT.

"How shall not the ministration of the Spirit be rather glorious?"
—2 Cor. iii. 8.

WHAT man does not yearn over the long-lost joys of his boyhood, when he remembers the merry game, the light heart, the cheerful circle, the holiday and the prize, the youthful love and the freedom from care which marked those early days? And yet we all honestly think that manhood is a nobler thing than childhood; that the cares which have worn wrinkles on the brow have been part of a heavenly discipline, and that the energy and pursuit of active life are greater gifts than those which are sunned over by the glow of life's bright dawn. Who does not yearn, amid the doubts and difficulties awakened by maturer judgment, for the simple faith with which, in his early days, he received all the statements that were made to him, when to hear and believe were one, when suspicion never clouded the face of truth, when difficulties and questionings were almost unknown? Yet those who have gone through the agonies of honest doubt, and have conquered, feel that the knowledge which springs out of such questioning, and the faith which can survive such a test, and the love that has passed through such a fiery ordeal, are worth more than the implicit faith or simple assent which never cost a mental pang, and was not bought at so high a price.

The springing corn, with its emerald glow of fresh young life, is glorious; but the rich harvest is rather glorious. A scaffolding is sometimes a thing of beauty, and it seems a mistake to destroy it; but the building which it surrounds deprives it of permanent interest, and makes us anxious for its removal. There is a strong disposition on the part of some people to praise the good old times; to cry out that they were better than these, to sigh after the return of a simplicity, a slowness, and weakness which modern inventions, improvements, and education have scattered to the winds, and to think that all things are tending to a crisis for which society in general, and themselves in particular, are unprepared. Yet no man of competent mind can take a large view of human affairs and events, and come to the conclusion that God's providence stands still, that humanity is on the decline, that the times of limited education, restricted commerce, slow transit, spiritual despotism, and triumphant priestcraft were better than these; or that humanity at any previous period of its history was so moral, spiritual, benevolent, right-loving, and religious as it is at this present moment.

There is, however, and always has been this conservative tendency at work in society, and the Christian Church has never been freed from it. Even in the days of Paul and Apollos there were Gentile Christians to whom the Christ had come so dressed up in Jewish garments that they were anxious to retain as much as possible of the older dispensation. Now, though there were at Corinth those who were more in danger from indulging their freedom and turning their religious liberty into philosophic licence than from clinging to Hebrew or conservative prejudices, Paul was not afraid—in spite of the imputations which the Judaizing spirit had brought against his teaching—to reassert with unflinching boldness the spiritual nature of that gospel which he had been the first to proclaim to them. He knew that truth was mightier than prejudice, that no real harm could come from the utterance of what he believed to be true; and so at the risk that some of his readers would misunderstand and abuse the sublime truth, and while he frankly admitted that the older dispensation was in many of its aspects a glorious heritage, yet he boldly maintained that the ministration of the Spirit was rather glorious.

Paul felt that when the Spirit of Christ wrought upon the inert, almost animal life of the world, man would become once more the image of the invisible God, human society would be incorporated into a living body for the Holy Spirit, and that then all mankind would be transformed into the everlasting "living temple" of the Godhead. Yet there were then, and there are now, men ignorant of the power of that Spirit. Many are saying, "Show us a sign that we may see and believe;" and seem scarcely to know whether there be any Holy Ghost. Let us endeavour, in response to this state of feeling, to bring out the meaning and power of the inquiry of the text, by contrasting, as Paul himself does in this chapter, the ministration of the Spirit with other ministrations which precede, anticipate, and rival it.

I. In order to understand the ministration of the Spirit, contrast the *Spirit* with that which is most often brought into comparison with it, namely, the BODY. We cannot understand what is meant by body, without answering the previous inquiry, What is spirit? nor can we reply to this question without settling in our minds something about the body which it inhabits. If we see several things, or parts of things, united to each other by some secret bond, and subserving some general purpose, we are accustomed to speak of them as a body, and of that secret intention or purpose as their uniting spirit. In the same way a crowd of persons in the street, an assembly of individuals instinct with a common idea or intention, are constantly spoken of as bodies of men, and their common object is the spirit which actuates them. This arises doubtless from our consciousness that we are ourselves compounds of many parts, organs, members, and passions, over the strange assemblage of which a presiding spirit rules. We *have* a body; we *are* spirits. The body is dependent on the spirit, not the spirit on the body; the body may perish while the spirit lives, the body may be still alive when the spirit is virtually dead.

Now, associations of men, when governed by strong principle, in view of great objects and ruled by those whose spirit is capable of being infused into all around them, are such bodies; and even the *bodies* of these fellowships have a great work to do, for without their aid, however strong the spirit might be, it would evaporate and be lost to the world. Paul very frequently speaks of the Christian Church under this image. He says that it is the "body of Christ," and that it is inhabited by the Spirit of Christ. There is, says he, "one body and one Spirit, even as ye are called in one hope of your calling." "As the body is one and hath many members, even so are ye one body in Christ, and every one members one of another." The body of

Christ has a great work to do. It has to hold as it were in sacred keeping the invisible Spirit of Jesus; it has to exhibit in its countenance His feelings, and in its conduct His will. It has to seek its food and support amid the circumstances and according to the laws of human life. It has, like every other "body," to take up and turn as it were into its own wonderful substance the proper kind of aliment that is adapted to nourish it; it has to bring the knowledge, the science, the business, the politics, the poetry, and the reality of life under the same Divine influence, to submit it to the power of the same Spirit; and in fact all these functions of man as well as all classes of men are baptized into one body. Verily the body of so Divine a Spirit must be the most glorious association and the most powerful existence in the world.

Under the Old Testament dispensation a similar but inferior body grew up from childhood to maturity in the Holy Land; and the revelation of God made through it consisted to a great degree in the rules that were assigned to this body. The religion of Moses and Samuel and Ezra might with reverence and truthfulness be termed a ministration of the body. It consisted of innumerable regulations for the external management of the individual, the community, the priest, the king, the temple, and the State. Implicit obedience to these laws was grand and glorious until the prejudices of Israel led them to suppose that the body was of more consequence than the spirit, and the form more precious than the power. It must have been an awful and sublime spectacle to have witnessed the first revelation of the Divine law and the accompanying manifestation of the Divine presence. It was a grand education in the best days of the Hebrew theocracy to trace the government of the heavenly King in His earthly kingdom; to witness the splendour of the ceremonial when the Lord in very deed dwelt with man upon the earth; when the temple in which He shone forth upon the eyes and hearts of men was fashioned after His own design; and when the body was fed by His own loving hand, clothed and adorned by His own absolute wisdom and unbounded resources. But just as this ministration to a body was glorious, the ministration of the Spirit exceeds it in glory; and directly that the body considers itself to be the chief end of existence, whether it be the body of a man, of an institution, or of a Church, the spirit is impaired and hastens to its end. The *man* who sinks into such a condition becomes a morbid valetudinarian, a slave of his poor body; the *institution* thus perverted becomes obstructive to the end that called it into existence; and the *Church*, Hebrew or Christian, which in gorgeous ceremonial, antique rite, or prescriptive usage substitutes a care for the body in place of all the weightier matters of law and gospel, is unquestionably quenching the Spirit of God. When the Spirit works upon us as individual men, it transfigures our whole nature, and supplies us with abundant principles for every action; and while it convinces us of sin, of righteousness, and of judgment to come, it puts the Divine law in our inward parts, and will make us love holiness, do justly, and walk humbly with our God. It will eat out the evil desires of the flesh by filling us with holy passions. We shall then never be satisfied with the most careful attention to the most venerable rule or use, but shall be moved to live a Divine life.

Again, we have many institutions and societies, the body of which has sprung into existence, we believe, under the direction and teaching of the Holy Spirit. In proportion as they are Christian associations and imbued with the Spirit of the Son of God, sanctified by His presence and existing for His glory, they are parts of His scheme of mercy for a ruined world. But if we in our vanity begin to regard the mere association as the end rather than the means, if we endow the body with the dignity and value which belong only to the Spirit, we utterly fail. Let us beware of making our own sanctuary or schools or organizations, our Church principles, or even what we believe to be our true doctrine, into our idols, the ends for which we labour. All these things are of priceless value and rich in glory; but the ministration of the Spirit excels them in glory. That out of which all righteous action, all holy enterprise, all manly zeal must constantly spring, excels them as the spirit excels the flesh and blood over which it rules. In the childhood of the Divine life it is very important to strengthen the spirit by the nutrition and education of the body; and there are many things that minister to the process: but the ministration of the Spirit, direct communion with the living God—with the Fountain of all life, truth, wisdom, and purity,—excels the dispensations of childhood, the prescriptions given to the infancy of our race. By forgetfulness of this, many a soul, many an institution, many a Church has sunk into lethargy, ceremonialism, and formality; has confounded little prescriptions with great principles, and has quenched the fire or silenced the voice of the Spirit of God. The ministration of the body, that is, the splendour and ritual of worship, the forms of holy sacraments and common prayer, the details of Church organization, of apostolic and other successions, may be glorious; but the ministration of the Spirit is rather glorious.

II. Contrast the *Spirit* with the LETTER. The simplest illustration of this antithesis may be found in the nature of language. Take any word you please. Write it down. Look at it. Of what does it consist? Of a few strokes only, which in themselves are utterly unmeaning. Pronounce the word. What is it? A sound or collection of sounds which have no meaning in themselves. All that you know, after you have looked or listened long, is, that you and others agree to represent certain ideas and feelings by that word; but there is no necessary connection between the word and the meaning: for the same word may convey ideas and suggest thoughts that are altogether dissimilar to different people or nations. Illustrations of this are unnecessary, even though some may be unwilling to grant it, so soon as the word or letter has been used to represent for them some of the most precious or august ideas. Thus, though the letter and the word have great value, they are transitory, accidental, liable to change; but the thing itself connoted, or the spirit conveyed by the letter, may have an undying worth, and be a permanent, an eternal truth.

We speak of the letter and the spirit of a law or of a testament. The one may be observed, while the other is violated. It is quite possible to break the spirit and fulfil the letter of the law of our country, or to respect the spirit and reject the letter of it. It is very easy to fall in with the injunctions of a dying man, rigidly to obey the letter of his instructions, and to violate their spirit and set at nought all his wishes. Often has the letter of the Divine law been scrupulously kept, while its spirit has been irreverently trifled with; and very often the spirit of that law has been established, while the letter has been discarded and set at nought. Thus a Divine Spirit penetrated and illumined the restrictions and rules of the Old Testament dispensation; the spirit of that covenant of God with man has been ministered afresh in the gospel of Jesus Christ, but the letter in which that spirit has been conveyed by Moses and by Christ has widely differed. At one time the nation and government of Israel were the form in which God's love to man and His providence over His whole Church were made known to the world; but now the holy nation, the peculiar people, are not enclosed by the mountains round about Jerusalem, are not fed with honey from the rock, nor cheered with the milk and wine of earthly prosperity; but they are found wherever hearts beat high with loyal childlike love to the Father and Ruler of the universe, and wherever the Son of God has been revealed to living faith. They are found in the general assembly and church of the first-born. The spirit has been preserved, the letter has been changed.

In like measure the principle and spirit of sacrifice were seen in the thank-offering and the burnt-offering. In these ceremonies were expressed the devotion, the reverence, the dependence of God's children as well as their sense of His justice. But the mode of expressing these things—the letter—has been changed. Where is the temple? Not one stone is left upon another. Where are the priest and the sacrifice? Now that He is come who is "the end of the law" they have "ceased to be offered." On the other hand, the spirit of sacrifice is not lost; the gospel of Christ is the ministration of that spirit to the world. It presents the highest conceivable form of sacrifice, of entire surrender to the Father's will, even though the great High-Priest who offered up the sacrifice found therein humiliation, temptation, near contact with the evil one, and the most awful form of death. Here is a complete propitiation, a perfect sacrifice, a noble testimony to the Divine holiness, a fearful exposition of the evil of sin, the most sublime incentive to self-sacrifice. The gospel is the ministration to us of the intensest spirit of self-sacrifice; it teaches us, as its spirit enters into us, to present our own bodies as living sacrifices, holy and acceptable unto the Lord.

Take another illustration : the idea of holiness, of consecration to Divine use, and separation from all contaminating influence, was traced out and developed into marvellous detail among the favoured people. It was possible for everything to be holy; not only were the priest and the people, the father and the child, the day and the place consecrated, but from the high altar to the bells on the horses, everything that men could use, every class of society, every duty, every hour of every day, every article of dress, had its own mode of sanctification. The most minute rule was given for every act, from the ceremony that consecrated a king or a priest to the humblest operation in a household. These rules have for the most part been superseded in the dispensation of the Holy Ghost. The letter has been laid aside by the infusion and sufficiency of the far higher principle of love to God. Yet the domain of holiness itself has not shrunk into narrower limits; we are not excused from the responsibility of being humble, conscientious, or consecrated in every relation of life, but the spirit of holiness now takes a far wider sweep, and gives us principles of action rather than rules for every act; we serve God in "the newness of the spirit, not in the oldness of the letter." The gospel of Christ supplies us with powerful motives, puts holiness before us on a higher elevation, exhibits it to our view in an embodiment of its loftiest perfection, and assures us that the same Spirit that was given to Him and that abode on Him is sent forth into our hearts, crying "Abba, Father." Let us not forget that the ministration of the letter was glorious. We shall not understand the dispensation of the Spirit unless we appreciate the real excellence of that which has been superseded and outshone.

The letter was glorious when it first of all clothed Divine thoughts in undying words and communicated them to men; but when the Word was made flesh, and the Divine ideal of humanity was no longer expressed in a series of sentences but in a perfect human life, the ministration of the Spirit surpassed the ministration of the letter.

The elaborate ceremonial of prescribed rules was glorious. "Beautiful for situation, the joy of the whole earth was mount Zion." "This is My rest for ever," said Jehovah, "here will I dwell, for I have desired it." The sacrifices which set forth the majesty of law, and the triumph of mercy; the priesthood which took the burden of the sinful heart into the awful presence and consumed it there with holy fire; the sabbath on which Israel entered into Jehovah's rest; the jubilee when the whole land reverted to the Divine Ruler,—were all glorious: yet it must have been a still grander sight to have seen some old Jewish priest—who valued his temple, his sabbath, the sacrifices that he had to offer, and the sacerdotal course to which he belonged, as deeply as his own soul—approach the gorgeous pile that crowned the heights of Zion, and declare, "There is One greater than the temple; there is a Sacrifice more precious than this costly hecatomb; there is a rest more holy than my sabbath; there is One who is the Word of God, the Word made flesh and dwelling among us; there is a glory that excels all that once enshrined for me the Divinity; the way unto my Father is now made manifest."

The same principle must apply to the contrast between the letter and the spirit of the gospel. Incalculably precious as this new letter really is, it must not be forgotten that it *is* letter, and that the spirit of the gospel far excels it in glory. The letter of the gospel may ultimately prove to be no less indefinite, no less imperfect, no less transitory than the letter of the Old Testament; but its spirit is eternal and can never exhaust its energy or lose its power. "The letter killeth, but the spirit giveth life."

Many are striving to bind down even the spirit of the gospel by prescribing rules of holy living, by special modes of expressing the Divine life, by logical inferences drawn from the revealing word, by the experience which has been sanctified in the Church, by words and phrases of our holy gospel itself. It is none the less true here, also, that though the ministration of the letter be glorious, the ministration of the Spirit is rather glorious.

III. Another contrast, and one which is still more frequently unfolded in the New Testament, is that between the Spirit and the FLESH. This contrast, upon which St. Paul dilates at great length in the Epistle to the Romans and elsewhere, involves a far profounder view of human character and destiny.

It is clear that by "the flesh" the apostle does not mean the mere physical system as opposed to the soul or to the spirit, but he refers to the fleshly nature of man. By the flesh he means the whole of our nature when left to itself, or, as he elsewhere expresses it, "the natural man." He means man such as he is when untouched by higher influences; man, when he is following the desires and is walking in the imaginations of his own heart. He means that which is born of the flesh and is flesh; the carnal mind, which is enmity against God and is not subject to the law of God. The apostle and the other writers of the New Testament mean by "the flesh" the mere functions, tendencies, and impulses of the human being, in unrenewed and unregenerate humanity, not such as God had made it, but such as sin has left it. We know that the society of heathendom in Paul's day was so bad, and the light of truth and the working of the Holy Spirit were so new and so much restrained, that it was necessary that he should dip his pencil in the darkest shades to give a true outline of the corrupt state of man. But even in the present day the higher faculties of man evince some of his worst characteristics; and poetry, science, philosophy, business, pleasure, when left to develop themselves without a Divine and controlling principle, reveal the lamentable anarchy of our nature and the miserable bondage of our will. It is with this flesh, this unregenerated humanity, that St. Paul contrasts the ministration of the Spirit, the life of the spiritual man. By the latter he everywhere means the result of the new creation within us, the setting up within a human soul of a new and Divine life by the Spirit of the living God.

By the "Spirit" as opposed to the "flesh" Paul means the dwelling in us of the living Christ, the overpowering and overawing of both the lower and the more cultivated passions of the soul by Christlike and heavenly longings; he means that expunging and renunciation of ungodliness and worldly lust, that strengthening of our inner man, that being rooted "and grounded in love," by which we both comprehend and "know that which passeth knowledge." The apostle by this phrase aims at nothing less than the completion of man after the completeness of Christ, the quickening of our whole spiritual being, and an alliance with God Himself.

The more we know of the gospel the more we see that it is designed and adapted to awaken and minister to the great change from flesh to spirit; that its prime end is to produce, to exhibit, and to complete it; that the Divine Creator-Spirit thus "pours His joys on human kind," thus renews and saves the soul of man, creating that which will find body and letter for itself. The gospel is "the ministration of the Spirit." It conveys spiritual blessings, not temporal advantages; eternal life, not human distinctions; the favour of God, not the praise of man; heaven, not earth; a new life, not a new dress; a new heart, not a new language; nothing less than "a new man after the image of Him that created him;" "changed into the same image, from glory to glory, even as by the Spirit of the Lord."

There are those who teach otherwise; who describe the gospel of Christ as only a new and enlarged edition of the self-instruction which the human heart and intellect have found for themselves in nature, in providence, in conscience, a mere ministration of the flesh, of the unaided nature of man, deprived of its heavenly origin, and robbed of its Divine attestations.

Now, we must not forget that the ministration of the flesh, including under that term all that the intellect, conscience, and will of man, unaided by the Divine Spirit, have ever been able to achieve, has been undeniably glorious. There is an appalling grandeur in some of the efforts of man. The daring of Prometheus, the wisdom of Confucius, the conscience of Socrates, the mental affluence of Aristotle, the insight of Plato, the self-sacrifice of Buddha.

and all the long and dreary effort which the flesh has made to crucify itself are full of wondrous sublimity. I do not say that there is no leading of the Spirit of God through all these forms of the ministration of the flesh, but they are powerfully contrasted with the dispensation of the Spirit.

We are awed and smitten dumb with amazement at the power of falsehood and folly to inspire enthusiastic reverence; we are confounded by the gorgeous fanaticism of the eastern world at work through untold ages, from the builders of the pyramids to the last processions in honour of Juggernaut; and we are at times anxious and agitated when we see the triumphs of a purely physical science that repudiates every possible mode of stating faith in the living God,—yet it cannot be denied that the whole ministration of *the flesh* has some glory of its own. Still, it has no glory by reason of the glory that excelleth. How much does the ministration of the Spirit excel the glory of all that attempts to rival it? The spirit soars into a region where the flesh in its most refined form cannot penetrate; it deals with problems that science is proving herself less competent than ever to solve; it induces in human nature a new series of forces and energies which transcend reason, satisfy conscience, sacrifice self, and glorify God.

IV. Consider, in the last place, the apostle's contrast between the ministration of DEATH and the ministration of the *Spirit*. The ministration of the *body* was a ministration of that which is perishable and must die, and hence it is a ministration of death. The ministration of the *flesh* is a ministration of that which has no real vitality in it, which does not draw its strength from unseen and eternal sources; and hence it too is a ministration of death. The ministration of the *letter*, of the law graven on stones, had a glory, but it was a ministration of threatening and warning and destruction, rather than of life. It possessed, however, a glory of its own, and when Moses descended with it from the secret place of the Most High his face shone with supernal radiance; but it was a glory which was to pass away, and the passing away of which was concealed by the veil that covered it. But the ministration of the Spirit is eternal in its character, unfading in its beauty, outlasting temple and tabernacle and veil. The law became a ministration of death. The thunder of Sinai, the fire that consumed the sons of Aaron, the plague and the earthquake, the fiery serpent, the raging sword, the destroying angel, and Death, the standing enemy of our race, became the awful ministers of the dispensation of God. These commandments were grievous, and though ordained ultimately for life were found to be unto death. Sin, taking occasion by the commandment, deceived and slew its victim. It is in contrast to this that the apostle describes the ministration of the life-giving Spirit; that Divine message from God to the human race by which the spirit of man, instead of being submitted to restrictions which cross its desires and aspirations, is expanded and developed into agreement with the mind of the Lawgiver,—instead of being wrought upon by a machinery designed to restrain its corrupt propensities, is brought under the influence of a power which shall inspire Divine impulses and desires.

The whole of the ministration of death had a glory of its own. The great Lord of life utilized the strange and mysterious law of death, and made it teach mankind lessons of life and happiness. The flaming sword of cherubim, the sepulchral waves of the deluge, the procession into the deep waters of death of kings, sages, and saints, of hoary patriarchs and prattling babes, the heroes of many times and peoples who, spite of their love of life, loved virtue and their country and their conscience more, were in and through death a sublime ministration of the law of the Most High. The bleeding victims on a thousand altars, and preeminently those which special revelation made prophetic of the great Sacrifice of Calvary, were a ministration of death that was glorious in holiness and fearful in praises. "When the burnt-offering began the song of the Lord began." The incense of gratitude sweetened the hecatomb. The glory was great, though it was terrible. The ministration of righteousness, the dispensation of the higher life, imparted through living faith in the dying and risen Lord, exceeds it in glory. As the sunrise is more glorious than the sublimity of the midnight storm, as the dayspring from on high is more glorious than the dazzle of the lightning or the sweep of the devouring hurricane, as the smile of spring and the fertility of summer are more glorious than the "autumn fire," than the magnificence of the iceberg or the gorgeous mirage of the desert, so does the ministration of righteousness exceed in glory all the ministration of death. We have, then, in these contrasts of St. Paul deep reasons for adoring gratitude, for profound satisfaction, for ardent holy longings. We may be stimulated by them to open our whole nature to the Spirit and to His mighty working. We may rest calm in the triumph which we know the Spirit will gain over the mere body, over the mere letter of our institutions or our dogmas; we may cherish an unwavering confidence in the ultimate victory of the Spirit over the flesh and over the doom of the flesh. "To be carnally minded is death, to be spiritually minded is life and peace."

THE TENTH BEATITUDE.

THE TENTH BEATITUDE.

"Ye ought . . . to remember the words of the Lord Jesus, how He Himself said, It is more blessed to give than to receive."—ACTS xx. 35.

WHEN St. Paul visited Miletus, and delivered his parting charge to the elders of the Ephesian Church, several of his own most potent letters had been already penned. These were saturated with thoughts the origination of which we cannot fairly attribute to him, and for which we can find no adequate explanation either in Hebrew literature, sacred or apocryphal, in Greek philosophy or Alexandrine theories. We read between the lines, ideas, principles and facts already taken for granted by St. Paul and his readers. He and those to whom he wrote had clearly moved into a new world. The veil had been lifted. The unseen had become visible. The way to the blessed life had been manifested. Both worlds were dominated for them by one Supreme Personage, who, though nothing less than God over all, "blessed for ever," had yet so taken up into Himself our humanity, had so glorified the dying and risen Christ, that every problem of life had been restated, every aspect of the world had been revolutionized, every ethical question that had distracted the schools of Athens, Ephesus, and Rome had received a new solution.

If the new faith cannot be fathered on Hebrew prophet or Greek sage, and was not then and there being wrought out and revealed in Paul's own consciousness—we must look deeper for an explanation of the great apostle's views of sin and death, of God and redemption, of salvation and life eternal, and of the God-Man Himself. Where can we find any explanation more rational than that Paul had been himself revolutionized by the "words of the Lord Jesus"? This much is historically certain, that when the apostle was making this memorable voyage, a society of men was rapidly coming into existence which embraced both the living and the dead, which enshrined the principles and caught the spirit of the Christ. This fellowship was built on the assurances and promises which were uttered in human words by Jesus Christ during the brief period of His sojourn on earth. Not more than a quarter of a century had elapsed since men still living believed that they saw Him, in the humanity that they loved, "pass through these heavens that He might fill all things." He was nothing less to them than the "wisdom of God" and "the power of God." He met the needs and the passionate yearning of Jew and Greek, of Oriental and Roman, of Barbarian and Scythian, of bond and free : Christ was said to be "all and in all."

Strange to say, from our modern standpoint—so far as we know—not one of the four Gospels had then been written, still less circulated. Nevertheless, the teaching of the Lord Jesus Christ had gone forth from the hills of Palestine into all lands. His words had moved "like the appearance of lamps" in Ezekiel's vision. They "went up and down among the living creatures, and the fire was bright, and the living creatures ran and returned as the appearance of a flash of lightning;" and "the noise of their wings" was as "the voice of the Almighty." St. Paul had clearly grasped and thrown into his own phraseology the thoughts and words that the beloved disciple subsequently recorded in the fourth Gospel. Moreover, we gather from his indubitably authentic letters, that those words of the Lord Jesus which are preserved by the third Evangelist—in (what M. Renan calls) the most beautiful book in the world—were ever in the heart and on the tongue of the apostle of the Gentiles; and that neither Matthew, Mark, Luke, nor John gathered up a tithe of these Divine words, which spread like prairie-fire round the whole seaboard of the Mediterranean.

The patristic contribution of these memorable sayings to general tradition is fragmentary but noteworthy, and within the last decade a previously unknown "word of the Lord Jesus"[1] has been let fall upon us as a drop of liquid light, of strange potency, and not without its bearing on the "Word" which is embedded in a form of crystalline beauty amid the admonitions of this farewell speech of the Apostle Paul. Many another word may there and then have been circulating like the visionary "wheels" of Ezekiel. Sometimes they burned like fire, and anon as they passed from lip to lip, from language to language, from heart to heart, they distilled Divine refreshment or poured themselves out in showers of blessing. We are conscious of no exaggeration when we say that we could more willingly part with many an ancient classic, with many an ode of Pindar or oration of Demosthenes, many a treatise of Aristotle or Cicero, whole sutras of Buddha and much Vedic literature, than with this Divine utterance which goes down to the very depths of human life, and stretches out to embrace the essential

---

[1] See the *Didache*, i. 6, and compare with Ecclesiasticus xii. 1-6.

blessedness of God Himself. Small and bright as a dew-drop, yet, as we watch, it swells into a veritable ocean of love, on whose placid surface are reflected all the glories of heaven and earth.

"It is more blessed to give than to receive!" Our Divine Lord said "*more* blessed." Then it *is* blessed to *receive*. Until we know the blessedness of "receiving," we cannot appreciate the higher blessedness of "giving." There is no antithesis here between the blessedness of giving and the *non*-blessedness of receiving. The comparison which our Lord made was between the greater and the less, between the higher and lower forms of blessedness. Oriental mysticism, Buddhist legends, have urged the hyperbole of self-sacrifice for its own sake, have stumbled into this veritable pit of pessimism. The Lord Christ illumined the profoundest problems of ethic and the true secret of the religious life, when He said: "It is *more* blessed to give than to receive;" "freely ye have received, freely give."

Let us ponder for a few moments the blessedness of *receiving* some of the richest and noblest things of human and Divine love. God Himself is the great Giver. His gifts are messages direct from His heart, and the Father's signature upon them brings Him very near to the minds that interpret this mystic handwriting. By receiving the bestowments of love, we enter into the mind of the Giver. If *we* cannot receive, *He* cannot give all that He is willing and able to impart. If the object of love fails to appreciate and appropriate the royal bounty, God Himself is wounded and pierced by the ingratitude. Hearken to the wail of the heart-broken prophet Hosea, a man who was inspired to weave out of his own infelicity and domestic tragedy a representation of the injury done to the Lord God by His faithless bride : "She did not know that I gave her corn, and wine and oil, and multiplied her silver and gold." "I have written ... the great things of My law, but they were counted as a strange thing." And again : "I taught Ephraim to walk, taking them by their arms, but they knew not that I healed them." Thus Isaiah also pleaded in the name of Jehovah with the men of Judah : "What could have been done more to My vineyard that I have not done in it?" And our Lord remonstrates with His hearers : "Ye will not come unto Me that ye might have life." Because we are too ready at times to get beyond our position of humble recipiency, we often fail of the grace of God. Some enumeration of these gifts may help to chastise our ingratitude, and disturb the pride that is anxious to earn and to merit grace, before it is roused to perceive our own utter helplessness, our mendicancy, our entire dependence upon the gifts, the tokens, and the amnesties of Infinite Love.

1. It is blessed simply to receive *Nature's* gifts even before we can apprehend their full complexity, their lavish abundance, their anticipation of our desires, their hidden secrets, and their boundless possibilities. All the progress of man is measured by the degree to which he has appreciated and received, discovered and utilized, the free gifts of God in nature. When man first understood what Nature had done for him in offering him the flower and fruit and seed of corn, then began the harvest of the world. When human intelligence apprehended what was involved in the chalk-beds and coalfields and mineral wealth at his feet; when he grasped the meaning of fire and lightning, and the contents of water and air; when he

thus received these treasured forces and boundless provisions of Nature; when he began to "receive" and utilize the energies which had been moulding the world for untold centuries,—then science took its birth. If we stubbornly refuse to receive the light of heaven, we stumble blindfold into the pitfalls at our side. Should we refuse to receive our daily bread, or put it from us with suicidal hand, we perish. Furthermore, Nature lavishes upon us together with these elementary gifts, appeals to our higher and more subtle desires, awakens them by her magic touch, and gives us the sense of beauty, truth, and goodness. The surpassing loveliness of much of Nature's work must be *received* by those who have the eyes and ears of the spirit opened to perceive it. All that ART has ever done to soften and beautify the career of man upon earth, has been to record the high joy, or subtle pain akin to bliss, which the perception and reception of the glory of Nature has given to a comparatively few elect souls. The great artists and poets, musicians and sculptors, have so embodied their strong emotions in abiding form and material, that others may learn from them the blessed secret of receiving the mystery of beauty, and accepting some of the truth and goodness of its eternal Source.

2. All human love is a ministration of Divine love. Human tenderness is but a channel cut by Holy Providence through which the rivers of God's pleasure flow. God lavishes His own love upon us through the hearts and by the hands of those who love. Now, it is blessed to receive *human love*, and the gifts of love. Self-sacrifice would be a form of selfishness, if it monopolized all the blessedness of the process. See the child with its hands full of birthday-gifts, intense joy lighting its eye, almost bursting the tiny

heart. If the little one had no blessedness in receiving father's, mother's, and sister's tokens of love, and found no joy in its new riches, if such were thrown idly away and conveyed no thrill of bliss, the grace of giving would be doubtful. Sometimes pride of spirit refuses to be beholden to another, resents the sense of obligation, groans over the necessity of accepting beneficence, cannot confer the higher joy on those who have the power and will to give. Perhaps the explanation is, that they desire to reverse the relations: they envy the power of giving the smaller blessedness to another. However this may be explained, it is an exception which illustrates the enormous spread of the rule, that it is "blessed to receive;" only on this principle can the inequalities of human power and capacity be compensated, can the strong help the weak, can the physician heal the sick, can the wise instruct the foolish, can the ignorant walk in the light of knowledge, can genius lighten care, and the great thoughts of a few become the bread of life to the many. Because it is "blessed to receive," we can drink into the spirit of the mighty dead, we can utilize their pregnant guesses and apply to our own case their hoarded wisdom. All beneficence would be dried at its source, all philanthropy and evangelism at home and abroad would sicken and die, if there were no blessedness in receiving the streams of living water which are always pouring forth from human hearts.

Is this too much of a truism to illustrate further? Perhaps the effort to do so at all would be superfluous if there were not lamentable forgetfulness of this principle on the part of some recipients of the noblest gifts of all. Are there not specimens all around us of ingratitude for blessedness already enjoyed and utilized? Are not parents sometimes broken-hearted because they never know the blessedness of *receiving* the confidence of their children? Are children always enriched as they might be with the blessedness of receiving the best gifts their parents could (if their minds were spiritual and unworldly) freely bestow? Do husbands and wives always find opportunity of rejoicing in one another's gifts? Are not kindness and sympathy often withheld where they might flood the parched heart with lovingkindness? Would not human life be indefinitely brighter, if many who were gorged with advantages lavished upon them by others, no longer ungratefully withheld from those to whom they owe so much the blessedness of receiving a faint recognition of the debt? Let us think of our great discoverers who have conferred joy on millions, yet have died in poverty and neglect; of the poets who have added sunshine to daylight, yet who have never found one beam of love to cheer their own dark lot; of the great patriots and statesmen who, age after age, are made the butt of malice, and are hated for their goodness; of the martyrs for liberty, truth, and righteousness, who have never known the blessedness of sympathy, and whose dying agonies have been mocked by prophecies of eternal hatred, and threats of everlasting fire. Such tragic indices of the stolidity and corruption of the human heart prove how imperfectly we recognize the blessedness of receiving human love.

3. Once more, the most impressive illustration of the principle is the veritable blessedness of receiving the grace of God. The secret of receiving from the living God what is neither earned nor merited, and, moreover, that to which we cannot lay the smallest claim; nay, further, that which we have madly, meanly, gracelessly forfeited, is a secret which some are slow to learn. Human pride comes in and

resents unmerited compassion, and disputes the necessity for mercy. Philosophy helps it to minimize the peril of sin, and a shallow science throws all the blame of sin on nature or matter or on God Himself. The blessedness of receiving Christ's supreme gift is disputed, because it involves too severe a self-scrutiny. The flesh which crucified *Him* once, resists the crucifying process when faith begins to drive the nails into its own quivering hands. The world must be crucified by the cross of Christ, but the world in our hearts dies hard. It is blessed to accept Christ as our wisdom, when we have once done it, but it is a bitter trial to confess that our own wisdom is folly. It is blessed to receive the Lord Christ as our righteousness, but the self-battle is often stern and long before we relinquish our own righteousness. It is life from the dead to find that Christ has redeemed us through the agony and death wherewith He accepted the full penalty and curse of human sin; but most of us have a fierce struggle before we admit our helplessness, or consent to the fact that "without Him we can do nothing."

It is blessed to receive what Jesus Christ gives to man, even though it smite down our pride and explode our self-sufficiency. We are blessed in this poverty of spirit, blessed even in our mourning, blessed in our new and heavenly hunger, blessed in the purging of the eye of the heart, blessed even when persecuted and reviled for such a faith, blessed though we are infinitely beholden to Him, blessed though it will take eternity to express our obligation or to pay "our debt of endless gratitude, still paying still to owe." It is blessed to receive the greatest gift, to receive into our very nature a new and endless life, to be born from above, to find thrilling within us the pulses of the

Eternal Love, and to know that we can take no honour, no credit whatever to ourselves for this Divine indwelling. It is blessed to sit in the sunshine of the Divine Presence, to behold the glory of the Son of Man, to be satisfied with the grace of the Lord Jesus, to be filled with all the fulness of God, and to be for ever with the Lord.

These golden words of Christ admit and enforce all this, but they authoritatively proclaim a deeper truth, and promise a blessedness that surpasses that of receiving from nature and human love their best gifts, or even that of receiving Divine grace. *It is MORE BLESSED TO GIVE than to receive.*

Can any reason be assigned for such a sweeping and comprehensive inversion of all ordinary maxims? Why should the bestowment of joy be a greater blessedness to the giver than to the receiver? Some tell us of the essential nobility of the disinterested affections. Others assure us that we are so constituted that we cannot have any real joy ourselves without imparting joy to others. Some dilate on the grandeur of human nature which invests sacrifice with this royal robe. Others undervalue this beatitude by regarding it as nothing more than a glorification of the golden rule. Is it enough to say that this is an ultimate truth deeper than thought itself? Will a wide induction of the so-called joys of earth and of unspiritual men confirm the statement? Should we not tremble to put it to such a test here in this Christian England of ours? Let the race-course and the stock exchange, the insurance office and the Parliament of England, the law-courts and the land-courts answer! Let diplomacy with its *Do ut des,* let trade and speculation, let professional etiquette and social distinctions and cliques be submitted to the fire of this principle. The honest advocate of such a law of life would be branded with scorn, and hustled off any stage of human activity. We need not travel to the Oriental seraglio, to the gangs of slave-traders, or to the battle-fields of commerce or of national rivalries, to the hells or slums of heathen cities, to see that ethical philosophers who try to find this great law of blessedness in a study of Human Nature as it is, have miserably failed. Our own daily habit and inward experience convince us that we are handling, in this profound and golden utterance, a state of things which *ought* to exist, but does not; which has not yet been adequately put to the proof, even within the society of the redeemed in the Church of the living God.

Have we personally acted upon this teaching even at the table of the Lord? Is it the regal principle at work in what calls itself the very body of Christ? Individuals may occur to us whose whole being is one unceasing process of giving, on whose brow there sits the dove of peace, and in whose eyes, which are full of tears of boundless sympathy, there gleams the light of heaven's own joy. But is their experience, their blending of apparent sorrow with sacred blessedness, a final proof? How can we justify this divine and prophetic utterance of the Lord Jesus? Is it a true law? Can we take the Son of Man at His word? The very form of the phrase seems to reveal the essential contrariety between Christianity and either Oriental self-sacrifice or Buddhist *Nirvâna*, which is now discussed by many who seem to do so in a spirit hostile to the religion of Christ. Buddha recommended the extinction of desire, the cessation of all yearning, utter quietism and invincible repose. Christ promised satisfaction to the highest desires, and He declared, moreover, which were the highest and the best.

He made such satisfaction a motive, He placed such joys as these before Himself, and He holds out to every faithful and loyal servant the privilege of entering into His own joy.

The judgment of the Lord Jesus was authoritative for St. Paul on this ethical and religious problem. The saying of the text must be true, and will be found to be true *because* He who is the truth uttered it. He must know. He came forth to us from among the sources and causes of all things. By Him and through His agency God made the worlds. He came out from God, and came into the world. He is more than a revelation, an unveiling of the truth. He *is* the truth, the reality and the complete expression, too, of human life and of Divine fulness. What He says about "blessedness" is of more weight than that which any other of the sons of men have said. He gave to the principle here involved the most complete expression. He tested it, as no other could possibly do, on the one hand, by a receptivity open to all the amplitude of the Holy Father's love lavished upon Him from eternity; and, on the other, by a sacrifice and gift of Himself, which was practically and to our most vivid imagination infinite and absolute.

He compared the eternal receiving and the infinite giving of His own experience with each other; and in the hour of His sorest travail, of His deepest humiliation, He seemed to say, "It is more blessed to give than to receive." This was His conviction, and He clearly made it the rule of His human life. The law of this blessedness was the law of His self-manifestation. In the wilderness He was tempted to use His supreme powers for the satisfaction of His personal requirements; He was tempted to receive miraculous sustenance and protection from disaster, so as the more easily to win acceptance from the sign-loving, wonder-seeking nation. He was tempted to receive the homage of the world by ceasing to wage warfare with the evil enshrined in it. He "suffered, being tempted;" but the higher blessedness of supreme self-sacrifice won the day: He gave Himself to life-long need; He consecrated himself to earnest, patient, and persuasive work. He gave Himself to the struggle with the world, the flesh, and the devil; to be crowned with thorns; to endure sweat of blood; to meet all the power of darkness; and He found all this *more* blessed.

When we are on the search for any ultimate principle, or for a sufficient explanation of some otherwise insoluble mystery, we always find ourselves driven to the same place of thought. *E.g.*, when we want to answer the question, "What is truth?" we never get rest till we find it in the presence of God, and learn that TRUTH, *per se*, is *that which God thinks about things*. If we yearn after a solution of the problem of the absolute BEAUTY, we can find it, not in the pleasure it gives, nor in the associations it summons, nor in the symmetry, nor in the resolved discords of the harmonies of nature, but in the robing, the vesture—indicating the near presence—of the Almighty. All beauty is but the cloud of incense round the shrine of His glory. BEAUTY is God's behaviour, just as TRUTH is His thought.

GOODNESS AND RIGHTNESS are never explained by such synonyms as "the beautiful," or the "true;" nor expounded by the unsatisfying dream that the "good" is the pleasurable; or that the "right" is simply the useful, profitable, or advantageous course of conduct. The conscience, the intuition of mankind, has never rested in that solution, nor does the mind ever feel at peace until it sees that the Good, the Just, the Rightful are simply names for the Supreme Being—for that which He is by His eternal nature. This shows us why all these terms melt into one when we press their meanings out into the Infinite. So if we wish to solve the deep meaning of our text, and ask why is it "*more* blessed to give than to receive"? we can only find the answer in the fact that God—the Eternal One and Three—is the great Giver. He finds His giving more blessed than His receiving; His Supreme Being is the witness to this, and so are His noblest acts.

A few words on each of these points.

The Eternal relation of the Father and the Son is the eternal interchange of giving and receiving love. There is a mutual affection in the depths of Deity. The philosophic and barren conception of a supreme, impassive, unalterable, impersonal MONAD strives hard to hold its ground, but Christianity has undermined it, and it will utterly vanish before the conception of God as "*Love.*" Before all worlds, before the angels were, or any force, or place, He was from eternity "Love." There was the perfect subject and the perfect object, and the perfect union of infinite Love: Father, Son, and Holy Spirit. In the text before us we see the very order of the Trinity. The Father's giving, *greater* than the Son's receiving. So Jesus says, "I and the Father are one;" but "the Father is greater than I."

The Godhead in the effluence of His glory is greater than is the reflection of that glory from the entire universe. From this principle we see some hint for the motive of the creation. The Lord called forth an object for the superfluity of His infinite Love. It was more blessed for Him to give than to receive, so the heavens appeared and all the host of them, and all the pomp of worlds. In this sense, to the glory of His great name, " they are and were created." From everything He *receives* some tribute, some reflection of His essential being, some echo of His word, some recognition of dependence upon His supreme will; but only from conscious mind can adequate response be made to love. From the love of God's creatures He receives an augmentation of blessedness, and so *Love* is the law for them, which if they break they introduce harsh discord into the music of the universe. Great is the joy of the Lord in the praises of His children, but greater still in bestowing upon them ever-abounding reasons for their praise.

The noblest and the most wonderful gift of the Lord God is the Incarnation of the Son of God, and that great act of the Father is the blessedest of all. He gave His only-begotten, His well-beloved. The fountains of the great deep of the Divine nature were broken up, but His joy was full. It was the joy of the Lord God Almighty.

But we must adapt this great principle of blessedness to the smaller range of our own experience, after seeing it tested in this flaming crucible of the Infinite Love.

Ye ought to remember and act upon *the words of the Lord Jesus*, because they express the whole manner of the perfect man, and the mind of the Lamb of God, and the very essence of the Eternal Godhead. St. Paul was apt at linking great and world-wide universal principles with our daily duties. *E.g.,* St. Paul will not prevaricate about his visits to Corinth. Certainly not. But why not? Because lies in the long run are disadvantageous or unpleasing? Nay; but *because* "all the promises of God are yea and Amen" in Christ Jesus. *Therefore*, Paul's "yea" must not be "nay." And so out of a law of life, as revelatory of the nature of God and the heart of Jesus as this is, St. Paul calls upon the Miletan elders to look tenderly after the weak and the erring. "*Ye ought to remember,*" because it is a truth you are, in the corruption and weakness of nature, in continual danger of forgetting, that it is more blessed to give than to receive.

I grant you all the blessedness of receiving the gifts of nature and of the world, and of the love of man: you must aim at the higher and greater blessedness of diffusing and conferring, of giving freely to others what you know to be worthy. The first believers sold their possessions, stripped themselves utterly that they might yield themselves to this sublime impulse, and know something of the blessedness of Christ, some of the blessedness of God. Many a saint and martyr has done the like, from St. Anthony to Basil and Gregory, Francis and Columba, and tens of thousands of those who have renounced all for Christ and His poor; all for Christ and those for whom Christ died. Ye ought to remember these words of the Lord Jesus when you are tempted to say: "Soul, thou hast much goods laid up for many years;" you ought to remember the words of Christ, when—to put it in a practical form—there is a question between the blessedness of buying a ring, or a picture, or a house, or a book, or a coat for yourself; and the blessedness of *giving* to the sick, the helpless, the naked, and the fatherless.

Most earnestly St. Paul counsels you to *receive* the grace of God, to receive the Christ, to receive the gift of the Incarnate Son of God, by a strong grasping of faith, in the implicit confidence of a perfect trust. This will make you blessed. Here is the blessedness of holy rest. With eyes suffused, with hearts aglow, you take the symbols of the body broken *for you*, of the blood shed *for you*. O, Christian believer, great is thy faith, great is thy blessedness! But art thou going to sit and sing thyself away to everlasting bliss? Nay, "Remember the words of the Lord Jesus." Ye ought to do so. There is a greater blessedness than this: you are to GIVE. Yes, to give yourself back to God in holy consecration. You are not your own, but you are His who has given Himself for you and to you. Human love is colourless unless it be mutual and ever-growing. Is love between the soul and Christ to be satisfied with lower levels and measures than the love of earth?

Lastly, we shall find the truth of our Lord's undying words when we enter into His joy. Heaven will surely not be the joy of an infinite and continuous recipiency, but the full comprehension of and the uttermost response to the Saviour's love. With all the saints may we comprehend the height, depth, length, and breadth of it! May we know that which passes knowledge, and lose ourselves in a supreme gift to Him! Not until we chant the endless hallelujah, not until we yield ourselves absolutely to our Lord God for eternity, having no will but His, shall we fully know how much more blessed it is to give than to receive.

ST. PAUL A DEBTOR.

Preached in the Chapel of Mansfield College, Oxford, January 18th, 1891, in aid of the work of the London Missionary Society.

ST. PAUL A DEBTOR.

"I am debtor both to Greeks and to Barbarians, both to the wise and to the foolish. So, as much as in me is, I am ready to preach the gospel to you also that are in Rome."—ROM. i. 14 (R.V.).

ST. PAUL himself preserved for the Church the priceless words of the Lord Jesus, that "it is more blessed to give than to receive." He implied in these very words, that it *is* blessed to *receive* the gifts of love, to receive the smile of reconciliation after estrangement, to receive the forgiveness of sins, the power and opportunity for service. What is there that we have not received? Christian experience undoubtedly turns upon the readiness of a man to receive unmerited and unearned mercy. It is "blessed" when pride humbles itself to receive an unexpected boon. We are pensioners on the bounty of the great Giver, and we are the daily recipients of gifts from a past which we cannot requite, gifts from our teachers and leaders, gifts from society which we have done so little to create, and from the noble hearts and bleeding hands of those who have suffered and died for us. It is blessed to receive all these things, but it is, said the Holy One, the Incarnate Word, *more blessed* to GIVE,—and He knew. Giving is more like God Himself, and is the very note or mark of His essential

Being. He is the fountain of life. He supplies all our need. He satisfies the desire of every living thing. The joy and blessedness of Almighty God is His infinite capacity to give us all that we enjoy, all that we need. Though He knows perfectly the blessedness of receiving the love, the appreciation of His children, the reciprocation of the Eternal Love, the homage of the spirits to whom He has given their life; yet He who came from His bosom, tells us that there are degrees even in the blessedness of God, and that, as between giving and receiving, there is no uncertainty: "It is *more* blessed to give than to receive."

This was also the experience of the Incarnate Love itself. He knew the blessedness of receiving the cup of cold water from one who was made happy by bestowing it. The breaking of the alabaster box of costly nard gave Him joy; *but,* it was more blessed in His esteem to give Himself, to surrender His all of earthly solace, to lay down His life as a ransom for many. Brethren of this Lord Jesus, believe Him and all His prophets and apostles when they teach you, by word and by example, that the fragrant essence of the new and Divine life is to *give* its best, to give its all, to give and relinquish itself to others.

Now, when St. Paul said, "I am a *debtor* to Greek and Barbarian, to wise and foolish," had he forgotten these words of the Lord Jesus? Did he find it necessary to fall back upon the sense of *duty*, in order to sustain the flagging energies of his love? No! The love which gives, is in its nature more blessed than the duty which prompts and urges us to some unwelcome task.

We do not deny that some cases may arise when even love needs the spur of duty, when "the stern daughter of the Voice of God" urges even the heart of love to do its best. Still, I cannot but think that when St. Paul used these memorable words, or when he said, "Woe is unto me if I preach not the gospel," the sense of debt to different classes of men was but the travail pang of an inward and overpowering love to his brother-man, which thus expressed itself.

The possession of a life-giving secret may, to a selfish and unrenewed nature, occasionally suggest nothing but personal advantage; and, at times, a limitless love may yearn and travail in the effort to express itself. The Samaritan lepers soon became ashamed of their selfishness, and they said one to another, "We do not well. This day is a day of good tidings, and we hold our peace: if we tarry till the morning light, punishment will overtake us. Now therefore come, let us go and tell the king's household."[1] So St. Paul felt that the whole world demanded from him the healing truth to which he had given the unqualified assent of his entire nature. He seemed to see the bewildered world, the Cæsars, the philosophers, the slaves, the cultivated few, and the toiling millions, rise from their places and take him by the throat, and cry, "Pay us that which thou owest." His sense of the brotherhood of man was becoming so strong, so intense in him, that he found that he had no right to retain these tidings of great joy to all people locked up in his own breast. The passion of his love to Christ and to those for whom Christ died constrained him; and so, in the sublime uprising of a love that was stronger than death, he said, "I am a debtor,"—"I am a debtor: I must pay my debt to old and young, to Greek and Jew, to Barbarian, Scythian, bond and free." Can we who glory in the name, in the teaching and life of St. Paul, catch a

[1] 2 Kings vii. 9.

little of his spirit? Can we take the world of men upon our heart, and, with the certitude born of living communion with the great Master and Lord of St. Paul, can we sting with the scourge of duty our transcendental sentiment into some definite lines of action? can we rise up out of our comforts and our culture, from our self-indulgent dallying with truth, and proclaim with a new and even passionate outburst of love, "We are debtors—we are debtors to Greeks and Barbarians, to wise and foolish. So, as much as is possible to us, we are ready to preach God's gospel of righteousness and love to every creature"?

When the proposal shapes itself in this practical form, some anxious thoughts arise within us, and tend to depress our enthusiasm. Can we offer the religion of Englishmen to the hoary East, when we are openly discussing whether we have a religion or not? Ought we to carry to the heathen world the assurance of a Divine Son of God, who is the Saviour and King of men, when here, at home, we often permit our message to evaporate into vague platitudes, and substitute ethical speculation for a revelation from heaven, and social proprieties for the religious life?

European thought, we are told, is suffering from violent transitions. It is said everywhere that we must adopt new platforms and new methods for the criticism of historic facts and literary survivals; and that we are in gravest doubt about the essence of our message. Can we, then, venture to break into the Oriental dream with our unsettled problems? Have we any truth worth uttering? Should we succeed in waking up the Brahmin or the Buddhist ascetics from their age-long sleep? At least, ought not our hands to be clean? Ought we not to compel our Government to abolish the opium traffic as a means of Indian revenue before we presume to teach morality to India or China? Should we not wait until adventurous traders cease to prey upon the passions of savages after gunpowder and ardent spirits? Would it not be rational to pause until the divisions of the Church are healed, and we have reduced our message to its simplest terms and forms, which no science will forthwith rush to analyze, and which will prove itself by its own proclamation to be true?

Our humble answer to this series of inquiries is, that if the principle had been adopted in other days, civilization and knowledge, science and history would have been strangled in their birth. If Newton had waited till he had solved the mystery of gravitation before enunciating its law, we might still have been learning scholastic astronomy. If Harvey and his followers had waited to solve all the mysteries of the circulation of the blood before proclaiming the luminous working hypothesis which has been so great a boon to medical science and practice, we might still have been floundering in the bog of mediæval medicine. Many analogous illustrations easily suggest themselves with respect to the same law of obvious duty. If St. Paul had kept his secret until the conflict between the synagogue and the Church had been determined, the marvels of the first century might have been delayed for a hundred years; and then it would have affected human destiny with a feebler touch and with diminished fire. St. Paul did not refuse to deal with the "waifs and strays" of Corinth until the philosophers at Athens would give him a more patient hearing. When Jews contradicted and blasphemed, and judged themselves unworthy of everlasting life, he turned to the Gentiles, and drew the dividing line between the ancient and the modern world.

Moreover, the differences among Christians orb themselves far less conspicuously in face of a dominant and fanatical heathen superstition than they do here, where they are often contending with each other and competing for general favour. After all deductions, the voice of the Churches and the message of Christendom is one voice, and one message is being offered to the world. Further, we cannot and dare not wait until the morning breaks, and until we have purified our own English life and washed out the stains from the national escutcheon.

Men often incorrectly estimate the direct message from heaven, which may and can be spoken by those who have seen the heart of God and who are sanctified by the Word and Spirit of the Lord, not by what it is in itself, but by the indirect effect of the Christian principle of a few upon society at large. Very slowly indeed has the standard of righteousness risen, even in Christendom. With tardy step has legislation been leavened with Christian principles. The wrongs of women, the traffic in slaves, private wars, fierce competitions, militarism, self-indulgence and vice on colossal scales have very gradually and partially yielded to the inward pulses of Christ's religion in individual hearts. Most certain is it that we have yet to see a Christian nation and, I almost dare to say, a truly Christian society. All the victories of the Cross have been won in spite of these odds. And the missionaries of Christ have always done their work against these tremendous difficulties; *i.e.* they have preached their gospel notwithstanding the fact that their ministry has been all along the line confronted by monstrous hypocrisies, and discounted by travesties of the faith. Lies, lust, greed, tortures, offensive wars, slave trades, tyrannies, persecutions wrought by so-called Christians have always cast their deadly shadows over the great enterprise. But hugely as these still loom to-day, they were never held so much in check, by the life of Christians, as they are at this hour. Nations know, as they never knew before, that these things are contrary to the mind and will of Christ, and must yield to His imperial voice, and they will not live even in the region of politics, or commerce, or diplomacy, or hierarchies, when once the Lord of men rises up to rule: "Be wise now, ye kings: be instructed, ye judges of the earth. Serve the Lord with fear, and rejoice with trembling. Kiss the Son, lest He be angry, and ye perish out of His way, when His wrath is kindled but a little." Our duty and our love join to tell us that, having learned the great secret of remedying the evils both of Christendom and heathendom, we have no option—we are *debtors* to Greeks and Barbarians, to the wise and to the foolish. Our love is not to be stifled by our difficulties, and we must put forth all the energy we have, to overtake the work that was left undone in the great ages of faith, and which has been left undone by our fellow-workers of to-day.

Some of the deeper questions to which I have referred will come more forcibly into view when we survey the two great classes of mankind to which, like St. Paul, we are debtors to make known the riches of Christ, debtors to offer the living bread, debtors to preach by life and lip the gospel of the grace of God.

THE GREEK AND THE BARBARIAN. Many who are sceptical about the message we have to deliver to themselves, have little to urge against missions to Barbarians, and heartily admit that it has been an immense advantage to the Samoan and the Sandwich Islands, to Madagascar and New Guinea, that they should be lifted even to the level of English Christianity. The story is often told of Charles Darwin's subscription to the Patagonian Mission. The Agnostic gives an ungrudging sympathy to the man who single-handed grapples with ferocious cannibals, tames them, wins them, clothes them, shows them how to live, teaches them the songs of the universal Church, and dies bravely at his post. Even the illusions of Christianity are to him a thousand times better than the delusions of the New Hebrides. Men like Livingstone and Moffat, Mackay and Hannington, Paton and Chalmers, receive the homage of those who can see that Barbarians are lifted from degradation by receiving the ideas of the much-decried Christianity of the nineteenth century. This result is not, however, the motive of the missionary. He looks beyond all the civilizing effects or literary results of the enterprise. Soul by soul, man by man, these Barbarians must be taught what manhood means. They must be put under the spell of Divine law, and be won by the Divine love. The fact that they know nothing of either, makes them the creditors of the apostle, the claimants for his secret. Their misery and hopelessness unconsciously press the claim. This is enough for any man who has caught the spirit of the dying Christ.

The fact is proved beyond doubt that the Negro, the Australian, Maori, and the Patagonian savage, the cannibal of the Islands, the hill tribesmen of India, the Malagasy, the Karens, the Pulliars, and the like, can and do apprehend the word and imbibe the spirit of the Lord Jesus Christ, and become so far imbued with the mind of Jesus, as to serve, to suffer, and die for His holy name. This is a commonplace of all missionary experience from the beginning until now. For the most part, St. Paul's dictum is demonstrably true, that God has chosen these "weak things of the world to confound the mighty, and things which are *not*, to bring to nought the things that are." For the most part, the vitalizing changes wrought by Christianity have originated in the lower stratum of society, and developed upwards until they have become conspicuous and assured. The muster rolls of martyrs contain, doubtless, a few illustrious specimens of sanctified culture; but for the most part they are the unnamed, the unknown, who were faithful unto death, and whose blood was "the seed of Christians."

This startling fact, in its degree, is still the great note of the Church in all lands. It justifies the fervent enthusiasm with which all devoted representatives of the Church do now throw themselves upon the lowermost classes of our cities, devising new methods to win them, seeking to preoccupy their minds with the ideas and impulses of our holy faith. The story of the noblest movements in the history of Christ's kingdom—those that have left the deepest traces upon Italy, England, and Germany—is the story of holy men, distinguished by high scholarship and burning hearts, who, in addition to their culture and grace and commission, have virtually said with the apostle of the Gentiles, "We are *debtors* to Barbarian and Scythian, to bondslaves and serfs, to waifs and strays: we owe them the payment of a debt which they have a right to claim at our hands." At this moment, nine-tenths of the missionary field is crowded with Barbarians, with savage races, with the uninstructed residuum of polytheistic civilization, with the victims of tyranny, of barbaric customs, of fierce passions and cruel vices. The Apostle Paul, the great confessors of old, the Catholic missionaries, the reformers of Christendom, our own noble society during the whole course of its history, from its Tahitian beginnings to its most recent triumphs in Africa, New Guinea, and Madagascar, have taken the same motto: "We are debtors to Barbarian and to unwise, to the downtrodden and to the slave, to the victims of our trade-juggernaut, to the ignorant and the foolish." St. Paul knew only too well that there were hordes and hosts of these *Barbarians* even in Rome itself, and that on his arrival there he might have to commence his evangelistic work with common soldiers, with jail-birds, with the rabble who clamoured for *panem et circenses*, with Tryphenas and Tryphosas, with freed men and fugitives; but he declared himself a debtor to the *outcast* in Rome, quite as much as to the saints in Cæsar's household.

This group of St. Paul's creditors, and of ours, does not exhaust his obligations or drain the affluence of his love. He was a debtor to the GREEK as well as to the Barbarian, to the cultivated as well as to the ignorant, to the wise and prudent as well as to babes. So when we acknowledge a similar debt to the thoughtful and self-satisfied Hindu, to the Chinese official, to the Japanese scientist, to the critical Zulu, to the esoteric Buddhist at home or abroad, we find our chief anxiety and difficulty. Few criticize our missionary propaganda to the Barbarian. They thank us for our work, and reap the harvest we or our fathers have sown, with no little appreciation of the martyr-like pioneers; but many scoff at our endeavour to bring the gospel of the Incarnation, the truth of the life and sacrifice and resurrection of our Lord Jesus Christ, to bear upon the literature, traditions, and theosophies of the Eastern world.

St. Paul believed with a profound conviction that he

had a message which would disturb the dream of the Epicurean, and the equanimity of the Stoic; he had facts to propound to the most diligent student of nature and man that could not be found among any of the Socratic sects. Paul was even passionately driven to pronounce sentence upon polytheism, and its moral malaria; and he dared to tell Platonist and Philonist that the relation between knowledge and virtue had not been solved by philosophy. He could speak of the invisible world and eternal life with a realism which only the Mysteries had attempted, and which they had confined to an initiated few. Paul was ready to reveal, to preach, that "unknown God" whom cultivated men were ignorantly worshipping, whether under the shadows of the Palatine or within the sight of the Athenian Acropolis. At the present hour, we have the distinct conviction that whatever truth is contained in the "Sacred Books of the East," that very truth is expressed with greater clearness in the Christian Scriptures; that whatever truth of moral order, whatever elevated conception of the character of God, or of Divine Incarnation, or of human apotheosis, or of union between God and man, has been dreamed of in heathendom is positively achieved and set forth in Him who was manifested in the flesh; that if the Fatherhood of God or the brotherhood of man has been faintly conceived or declared in the highest developments of non-Christian literature or observance, these principles have received a culminating and demonstrable expression in the life and death of our Lord; that the whole theory of redemption from sin, and of true sanctity, of conversion, salvation, and deliverance, is verified, and that we are bound to make it known; and that the whole method and principle of contact and communion with God through faith in Christ infinitely transcends all the methods of Oriental religion.

Most certainly, unless our gospel will stand this test of detailed comparison with all that other religions have to offer, either in their heroic history or their present fruits, our missionary enterprise will collapse. We would not offer our gospel, even to the Barbarian, unless we could confidently press it upon the wise and prudent, upon the most thoughtful Hindu and Buddhist, upon the proudest Confucianist or Moslem.

This is neither the place nor time to institute the comparison, but we have no shadow of doubt that, when Christ is brought, in the lustre and uniqueness of His own consciousness of His own work and claims, into direct comparison with the supreme *man* of every other faith, He will prove to be the Lord of all, the King of these kings of men.

The upshot of our meditation is simply this, that if we are alive to God through Christ, if we are irrefutably convinced of the truth about man given to us in His life, cross, passion, and glory, we must throb with a holy impulse to disclose a secret so life-giving to ourselves and one which affects the whole human race. Because the gospel of Christ deals with most universal facts of human nature, and bears upon the destiny of every human being in all time, we can trust and obey it for ourselves.

The missionary spirit and enterprise become powerful auxiliaries to the proof of our holy faith. We see in them an expression of that which is most essential in Christianity. If, with our present knowledge, we could have stood by, when the first man revealed the consciousness of his relations with the Supreme Being and Law, we should have discovered the highest revelation hitherto made of the glory and nature of God.

If we could, with our present apprehension of the history of the world, have listened to the intercessory prayer of the Lord Jesus, or watched His dying agony or heard His last words, we should never have doubted again that the Word had been made flesh, and that His glory was that of the only begotten Son, full of grace and truth. In fellowship with Him, we still feel that we have the one secret of life that is worth possessing. When we come face to face with the supernatural marvels which the truth about Christ works in human hearts, amid all kinds of men, and when we witness with our own eyes the miraculous change which declares that a man is reconciled to God, and has entered His kingdom, we too become more alive to God, and begin to live in both worlds the life eternal.

This missionary spirit, and this consequent strengthening of Divine life, is not *confined* to youth or maiden, to veteran or to pioneer who has given up an entire existence to the enterprise. It should be the spirit of every Church, of every Christian college, of every *individual* who professes or calls himself a Christian. It is the most vivid form of consecration to God, and the most certain sign and seal of the blessed life.

While yielding ourselves to its Divine captivation, we cannot despair of any human soul. Circumstances may degrade, pride may stupefy, self-indulgence may paralyze, doubt may bewilder, superstition, tradition, evil habits, inherited vice may check our hope; but we know that in the knowledge of the only veritable God and Jesus Christ Himself, the Apostle of God and High Priest for man, we have *eternal life*. There is no spell which has been wound about a human soul which will not vanish before the light of the knowledge of the glory of God in the face of Jesus Christ. No greater blessing can enrich our life than a mighty hope for our brother-man. In cultivating, in sustaining, the missionary spirit and hope, we catch a glimpse of the sunrise that is lighting the horizon of time, and we are preparing "the dawn that is spread upon the mountains." None have penetrated the invisible so far, or are so sure of the heart and of the power of the Son of God, as those who are verily acting on the motive which mastered the great apostle's ministry, and who can do no other than cry, "We are debtors, we are debtors to Greek and barbarian, to wise and unwise, insomuch as we are ready to proclaim the gospel of an infinite and righteous love to every creature."

The dawn of the eternal day will break over the earthly life of that young heart that consecrates itself to this high service. Brethren, you have but one life to live. To-day it is yours to give it to the grandest work that is being done among men. To-morrow you may have passed the crossing of the ways. Consecrate, then, this precious treasure to the noblest service, for our Lord Christ's sake.

THE SEED OF THE KINGDOM.

Preached at East Parade Chapel, Leeds

THE SEED OF THE KINGDOM.

"And He said, So is the kingdom of God, as if a man should cast seed upon the earth; and should sleep and rise night and day, and the seed should spring up and grow, he knoweth not how. The earth beareth fruit of herself; first the blade, then the ear, then the full corn in the ear. But when the fruit is ripe, straightway he putteth forth the sickle, because the harvest is come."—MARK iv. 26-29.

THE parable of the Sower, as it is given by each of the three Evangelists, commences with the words, "Behold, a sower went forth to sow." There is no introductory phrase whatever. It is true that, when expounding the parable to His disciples and those that were with Him, our Lord characterized the seed as "the seed of the kingdom;" but he made no such reference in the original utterance of the great enigma. Now, it is not to be supposed that among the vast crowds who waited on Him, those only who remained behind for further instruction gained glimpses of the meaning of His discourse. The image was one frequently used by classic and Oriental writers, when discussing the relations of the teacher to the taught.

A Galilæan crowd, accustomed to the use of figurative language, would perceive at a glance some part of the great Teacher's meaning; and since many among them were "wayside hearers," and others resembled the dry shallow soil upon a rocky place, the sense of disappointment may have thrown a cloud upon their faces, while their feelings ran in this fashion—" What has this to do with the kingdom of God? We want some manifest visible assurance that *that* kingdom has come nigh unto us; 'we would see a sign from heaven.' All that this Man has said to us, as yet, describes merely the relation of the Teacher to the taught; there is no special reference to that kingdom which all our prophets have taught us to expect, to the scene of its splendours, or the method of its growth. Why does He not tell us how He is going to establish it? Let Him take to Himself His great power and reign, that we may flock to His standard and crown Him king of the world." Perfectly true, there was no direct allusion made to the kingdom, no sure promise of its approach, and no explicit definition of its form; but, there was a prior truth, one that His hearers failed to recognize, one apart from which there can be no visible kingdom at all. Nevertheless, the Redeemer of the world, from His knowledge of what was in man, seems to compassionate this earnest cry of disappointment, and proceeds to show, that although the point of His first parable only referred indirectly to the establishment of His kingdom, and though the resemblance which He instituted only concerned that between the activity of seed and certain well-known realities of the spiritual world, and though it was used in the main to illustrate the responsibilities of the hearers of His gospel; yet the image itself was capable of new expansion. The parable of the Sower might yield at His touch royal similitudes, and be made to give forth the trumpet-peal which would usher in the advent of their King. Therefore was it that, according to St. Mark, He exclaimed, " *So is the kingdom of God, as if a man should cast seed upon the earth.*" That little word " so " appears to me to indicate that some conversation took place here, that some break had occurred in the thread of discourse, that some inquiry had been made, not unlike that which I have suggested, and which not only evoked the parable, but its Divine interpretation. Our Lord seems to say, " However striking may be the resemblance that exists between the sowing of seed upon different kinds of soil and the preaching of truth to men, there is a still more powerful resemblance possible between the action of seed and the establishment of the kingdom of God in the world." A clear perception of this purport of the parable may remove a difficulty which suggests itself concerning the agency here represented by "THE MAN" who casts seed into the ground.

If the reference be simply to the agency made use of for the dissemination of Divine truth, then the first part of the parable is quite comprehensible, but the last part becomes obscure. In what sense is "the man" who sows the seed to put in the sickle and gather in the ripened harvest? On the other hand, if "the Son of God," the true Lord of the harvest, is indicated, how can it be said of Him that *He* knows not how the seed grows and germinates? This difficulty has perhaps arisen principally from failing to perceive that it is not one single sowing of the seed, upon one class of hearers, that is spoken of here, but the whole of that sowing to the end of time—a sowing in which Christ participated for a short period during His earthly ministry, but which He then entrusted to those who had accepted His mission; while "the harvest" represents the final consummation of the kingdom, in which it will be His prerogative to act exclusively and alone. The image would have been obscure, if, when the great Teacher intended to indicate the mighty agency which should be employed for the establishment of the kingdom of God in the earth, He had made use of an illustration which in that period of history could have been applicable only to Himself, while He shows that the final development of the whole is pointed at by alluding to the great harvest, to the sickle of Divine Providence and Judgment, and to the granaries of heaven.

There are, then, more reasons than one for attending to the opening words of this parable, "And He said, So is the kingdom of God, as if a man should cast seed into the ground."

The parable as a whole suggests (1) The adaptation of the seed of the kingdom to the condition of humanity. (2) The law of its development. (3) The ultimate result.

I. The adaptation of the seed to the condition of humanity. "He said, So is the kingdom of God, as if a man should cast seed upon the earth; and should sleep and rise night and day, and the seed should spring up and grow, he knoweth not how. The earth beareth fruit of herself; first the blade, then the ear, then the full corn in the ear. But when the fruit is ripe, straightway he putteth forth the sickle, because the harvest is come."

Christ appears here to occupy the position of the first Sower. He is the first link of the mighty chain of agency that He was calling into existence, by which the sublimest truths about God should be brought into contact with human hearts and human society. By "the earth," I conceive that He meant, not any individual mind, not any one assembly of men, not any particular congregation or community, but the human race. He referred to all the instincts, habits, tastes, opinions, philosophies, and institutions of mankind, even to the uttermost limits of place and time,—to the whole of that vast and complicated structure which can be directly or indirectly permeated and affected by the truth of God. Such a conception of the "earth" on which the seed of the kingdom would be cast, was adapted to draw the minds of His hearers away from their national prepossessions and prejudices. They would obtain more comprehensive views of the true kingdom of God, if they could once deign to accept the idea of a *kingdom* which was based upon *truth*, of the victories of a King which would be gained, not by armies, but by the proclamation of the amnesty of heaven, if they could appreciate the foundations of a kingdom laid by a process so apparently inconspicuous as the preaching of a great gospel. Christ teaches us that, in addition to all the mighty human impulses that are germinating in society, and in addition to all the kingdoms that are arising in the world, and independently of the sovereign power that exists inherently in the large conceptions and fertile discoveries and creative intelligences of every age, there is the seed of another kingdom, which is not of earthly origination nor of human creation, and which, wheresoever it germinates, creates a province of the kingdom of God. "The kingdom of God is as if a man should cast seed upon the earth." By a man casting seed into the ground, sleeping and rising night and day, and in ignorance of the processes by which the seed springs up, Christ pointed to the whole of that human agency by which the truth of God shall be sown in the ground of humanity. It is indeed a Divine seed of awful potency and glorious possibility, but the sowing of it is entrusted to human hands.

The germination and development of the kingdom of God in any class of institution, character, or thought must necessarily be effected through the exertion of its influence on individuals. Now the processes by which these things are accomplished are profound and often inscrutable. Nothing is more manifest to the sower of the seed than the transformations which occur in individuals and communities under the influence of this truth ; but where, when, and how the result has been produced, "he knoweth not." The effects can be traced, the results are patent, but the seed springs and grows up "he knoweth not how." Verily, all workers who *do* so much, and *know* so little, are virtually warned by this parable not to be searching at the roots, not to be over careful about results, nor self-tormented about the final issues of the sowing. As men, we know no more about these things than does the husbandman who has cast seed into the ground, and leaves the wondrous influences of sun and shade, of dew and zephyr, of frost and rain, to co-operate with the pent-up forces of the seed, and bring about the divinely predestinated result.

"Sleeping and rising night and day" simply alludes to the withdrawment from the scenes and avocations of daily life of the Christian worker. It tells us how the sower leaves his seed with God, incapable of taking another co-operative step in the process of its germination. There may be in it a remote reference to the Son of Man as the Head of this human agency. If so, it was of His humanity that the parable speaks : and a dim prophecy perchance is involved of the solemn sleep of His death, a hint given even of His withdrawment to the scene where, though not constantly watching and tending the seed, He is engaged in pouring out the Divine influence on which all results are dependent, by which alone they can be accomplished. It is only in this sense that *He* can be said to leave the seed to itself; not indeed without the daily supply of His spiritual power, nor without the quickening sunbeams of His providential favour and the gently whispering breath of His Spirit; but, though " present " by the power of His Spirit, the manifestation of His humanity is suspended. He is hidden in the light of God. He would have us to understand that He is waiting for the results of His work, expecting the harvest of the world. So far as it is true that He will come again to us, He is now absent. In proportion to the fulness of His ultimate triumph and the glory of the final display of His interest in us, and of His great manifestation when every eye shall see Him, we must regard this intervening period, in which He is hiding Himself from our gaze, as an *absence*. He has gone His way. He will come again. We have no question at all that the harvest of the world will ripen, that the powers of conviction will become irresistible, that the manifestation of His true nature will eventually be so conspicuous and transcendent that every eye will see Him. But we cannot say this yet of any single generation, since the gates of heaven closed behind Him. If we contrast the ages of delay with the sublime fruition of all our prophetic hopes, we must say with the angels, " He is not here." The seed is sown, the great Sower is waiting to return to the harvest-field. Meanwhile, "the earth bringeth forth fruit of itself." In the earth there exist all the elements which subsequently contribute to the substance of the corn; in like manner there are existing in human minds capacities, ideas, feelings, and tendencies which are being reconstituted by the truth of God. Faculties and possibilities are lying dormant in human life and society, just as the carbon, nitrogen, and various salts that contribute to the material of the grain of wheat lie in the earth unused and unproductive ; but when the power that can attract them from their lurking-places comes into contact with them, they organize, act, and re-act upon one another, and as they show the signs of combination and life, they prophesy a happy future.

The idea which Christ suggests here, is the exclusion of the agency of the Sower from this part of the mighty process. The heart of man finds in the truth of God something essentially adapted to give life to the dull, apparently inert, materials of which it is composed. Human society finds in the truth of the Church of God the combining organizing power by which it is eventually to become the kingdom of God.

II. The parable is still further pregnant as it reveals the law of the development of the kingdom of God. "First the blade, then the ear, then the full corn in the ear." This is a beautiful illustration of the different stages of spiritual growth, somewhat akin to the division by the Apostle John into "little children," "young men," and "fathers;" and by the law of interpretation which we think we have discovered, we are bound to consider it the law of the progress of this new life in the history of man and in the records of God's Church; yet the exhibition of this law on the grand scale is the consequence of its truth in the history of every individual man who brings forth fruit with patience. It is because fresh life and infant life is poured into our world every day, that the whole world is ever young; it is because there are always children among us, learning the results of previous centuries of toil and labour and discovery, that the whole race is ever advancing; it is because there are young men who combine the vigour of youth with the resolution of age, the fire of enterprise with the calm maturity of fruition, that the world is ever strong, and marches forward towards the fulness of its prime. And it is because we see everywhere God's masterwork, man, the man of mature years with his strength and his knowledge, his wild fancies converted into the energy of imagination, his hasty prejudices chastened or uprooted, or in some cases perhaps dignified into well-reasoned opinions, his character rich with virtues, and his whole existence bearing witness to the life he has lived, that we anticipate the day when the entire human race shall have reached such a manhood, when the toils, illusions, and disappointments of the world's youth, the discoveries of centuries, the failures and martyrdoms encountered in the prolonged search after truth, shall issue in the full communion of humanity with nature, and the blessedness of the bridal between heaven and earth.

That which happens in the great world of men becomes a parable and type of the Church and kingdom of God on earth. The birth-cry is ever sounding, babes in Christ are being born continually into the kingdom. The regeneration of men is not a dream, but a blessed reality. The little children of grace, with their new fresh energy of wondrous beauty, their youthful charm and hopefulness, as yet the victim of no heart-breaking disappointment, souls sanguine but yet docile, make and keep the Church of God always young. Moreover, new fields of holy service are always being covered with the spring verdure of newborn hope. The Church has never yet lacked the ardour of fresh enterprise, the charm of new anticipations, the inspiration of the young life of the newly born.

Similarly the Church takes a character, as the world does, from its fully developed life. To every heart in which Divine life has been implanted, there must come the hour of conflict, of struggle, of temptation, of doubt, of fear; when faith trembles, and the first credulous confidence of the child is staggered by the cynical and sceptical voices of the unregenerate world; when that which is taken on trust has to be proved to the satisfaction of the intellect; when youthful glories of child-like faith become the intuitions of divine certitude; when, after having believed that it might know, a higher experience believes because it knows; when manhood, strength, experience, fruitfulness, characterize the Christian life. What is true of the individual gives a character to the whole Church. The kingdom of God is always youthful, but it is also always manly. It has always been characterized by childlike simplicity, but it is always throwing off the follies of childhood. It presents, like the tropical fruit-tree, at one and the same time the tender green of spring, the expanding blossom of summer, and the ripening fruit.

It would be well for the critics of the infantine simplicity of the faith of God's elect, to look more steadily at the manly force and vigour with which the Church is ever being taught of God to discard its own prejudices, to grow in grace and in the knowledge of our Lord Jesus Christ. It would be equally wise for those who are trembling at the signs of its vigour and aghast at its claim of glorious liberty to turn and see how fresh and beautiful and untarnished are the buddings of its early promise, and the childlike ways that "mark the newly born."

Once more, the man of God at last weathers all the influences adverse to his faith. He becomes a "Father in Christ Jesus." The hour arrives when old temptations are powerless and the perplexities of his prime have vanished, when the fascination and exaggerated importance of this world dwindle into insignificance and its pleasures fade away before the brightening vision of heaven. Then hoary hairs become a crown of righteousness, and we see standing on the shore of the river of death a goodly company attired for their passage, catching on their brows the reflected light of heaven. Our eyes brighten as we see them, for they give an earnest and prophecy of that condition of the CHURCH when the last conversion shall have taken place; when none shall need to say to his brother, "Know the Lord," when all shall know Him from the least to the greatest; when Jew and Greek shall have ceased their contentions; when Paul and John shall have finished their work; when no Stephen and no Polycarp shall need to seal a testimony with blood, and no mere worldly patronage shall threaten the spirituality of the kingdom of Christ; when the last conflict with Antichrist shall have been victoriously completed, and the whole world shall have become one vast company of fervent diligent workers; when the silver cords of prayer which bind this world to the throne of God shall contract, and earth, with its mighty burden of harmonious sympathies, shall rise—rise heavenward, until all that intervenes between time and the beatific vision of eternity shall be the thin transparent glass of the few moments of probation which yet await those "that are alive and remain," and which the trumpet of the Archangel shall shiver into fragments. "First the blade, then the ear, then the full corn in the ear," is the law of development for the kingdom as well as the man.

III. The parable exhibits in the circumstances of the harvest the ultimate issues of the kingdom. "When the fruit is ripe, straightway he putteth forth the sickle, because the harvest is come."

It is true of the man, and true of the kingdom of God as a whole.

When the whole fruitage of the Divine life is complete, the great Lord of the harvest, who alone has the power of life and death, puts forth His sickle. He alone knows the reaping time for souls. With Him are the issues of life. He uses His power over all flesh, and His dominion over all souls, with sublime independence of our foolish criticism, with infinite tenderness and perfect wisdom. When the fruit is ripe, then He puts forth the sickle. Sometimes the young and tender plant shows all its fruit, and He sees all its possibilities, accepts graciously unfulfilled intentions, and garners the bare promise of a glorious summer. But there are those who bring forth fruit in old age: and not till they have finished all their course does He take them into His arms and reap the shock of corn fully ripe. And we may rest assured that the great harvest of the world will be reaped by the same command, when the hour of its full fruitage shall have struck. He waits patiently. Henceforth He expects. He will see of the travail of His soul and be satisfied.

Far from us be the dastardly fear that the harvest of the world will never ripen, that the difficulties in its way are insurmountable, that the rampant growth of Oriental heathenism will never give way, that the blight of scepticism will destroy all the flower of the field, that the powers of the world will trample all the golden grain into dust. God has eternity to work in, and can wait; but the day will dawn when the harvest will be ready to His hand, and then immediately He will put in the sickle, not to destroy our hope, but to fulfil His promise.

THE IDEAL AND STANDARD OF CHRISTIAN UNITY.

Preached at East Parade Chapel, Leeds.

THE IDEAL AND STANDARD OF CHRISTIAN UNITY.

"That they may all be one; even as Thou, Father, art in Me, and I in Thee, that they also may be in Us; that the world may believe that Thou didst send Me."—JOHN xvii. 21.

EVERY word of the high-priestly prayer affords thrilling insight into the unique consciousness of our Divine Lord. These audible communings of Jesus with the Father reveal facts which transcend every other human experience. They expound the Incarnation; they provide a part at least of the reason which led St. John to set forth, as the presupposition of his Gospel, that "the Word who was God, and was in the beginning with God," "in whom was life" and "light," actually "became flesh, and took up His tabernacle amongst us." They prove that "He who was in the bosom of the Father, as His only-begotten Son, had indeed declared Him." The world had never known the Righteous Father, nor apprehended the opulence or the righteousness of God's eternal love to the humanity whom He made in His image. The Son of God, the responsive object of the Absolute Love, alone comprehended its supreme essence. "No one knoweth the Father save the Son," and "I (said He) have known Thee." Therefore He alone had power to declare the Name, and glorify it in full sight of the men who were given Him out of the world. Astonishing personal differences characterized these men. The morbid doubtfulness of *Thomas;* the eager credulousness and impulsive heroism of *Peter;* the yearning of *Philip* for a vision which, unperceived by himself, had already been granted to him; the despondency of *Judas* (not Iscariot) because no crushing or convincing effect had been produced on the hostile world around them; the silent mysticism suppressing the passionate intensity of the best-beloved *John;* the flashing fire of that other "son of thunder" who would be the first to drink His cup and follow Him through mortal agony into the thick darkness of the great light; the Messianic literalism of *Matthew;* the patient meditations of *Nathanael*, that Israelite without guile; the dreams of the political zealot *Simon;* the brotherly love and practical sense of *Andrew;* and finally the self-repressing modesty of the son of Alpheus, ever lost in the greater honours of his brethren and namesakes,—made the incomparable eleven, types of the whole of redeemed humanity. These all stood or kneeled around Him as Jesus poured forth this wondrous monologue.

Profoundly dissimilar in temperament, education, and capacity, they were bound to each other by their personal consecration to their Lord. He loved them to the uttermost, and they constituted a veritable brotherhood, a crystalline unity of many facets, each refracting with more or less of perfect colour some of the manifold rays of the one great light of the world. The apostles were not the sole objects of the intercessory prayer. There arose before the consciousness of Jesus numberless hosts of those who would believe on Him through their word. The desire of

His perfect love embraced these also. He prayed that they might become one in Him, that Jew and Greek, male and female, bond and free, should all be one, that every contradiction and antithesis should be resolved, that all individualities should be blended into one all-conquering unity. Thus only would the world believe that the Father had sent Him.

We can never read the prayer without a deep sinking of heart, because from the first day until now the gospel of the perfect love of God to man seems rather to have accentuated the natural antagonism between man and man, to have proved a sword of division as well as the message or implement of peace. Nothing, so it might seem, has more pitilessly separated chief friendships and divided hearts that otherwise, like kindred drops, had blended into one. A man's foes have been those of his own household, two against three, three against two, Communities bearing Christ's beloved name have been cruelly rent into fragments. Church against Church, heretic against heretic, Catholic against both alike. On every question touching the idea of God and of man, of the Christ Himself and His work, of the mission of the Spirit, of the organization of the Church, nation has risen against nation, the East and the West have ceased to hold communion with each other, and these in their turn have vied with one another in exasperating persecutions, ceaseless divisions, and bloody reprisals. Who dare say that any single fraction of the divided body has been free from moral blame and judicial blindness? The story of every century, from the second to the nineteenth, has emphasized in its degree, and on well-ascertained grounds, the fact that the Lord kindled fire and sent a sword upon the earth. The very means which were professedly adapted to harmonize and combine have been the most potent in dividing hearts, in arresting and quenching the Spirit. There are no pages in the sad history of the world more humiliating and deplorable than the records of sacrosanct councils and rival ministries, than the clash of swords over the meaning of the sacraments, ceremonies, and creeds of the Christian Churches. Volumes are needful, as we all know, to present a full picture of the passions which have been fostered and the crimes which have been committed in the name of Him who prayed in the last night of His agony that all who loved Him and believed that He came out from God might be *one*. Nevertheless, these dividing and colliding forces may receive some explanation when we review for a moment the disintegrating tendencies which have been always at work in humanity.

Consider the causes of disunion existing in the nature of human life and mind. Confusing differences of language, hereditary characteristics of race, the measureless influence of climate, soil, and food, combine to induce Jew and Greek, Chinaman and Saxon, Barbarian and Scythian, bond and free, to pursue different ideals. Within the limit of a single nation the divergencies of sentiment are violent. Political rancour hardly exceeds in virulence the exasperation that scientific philologists and different schools of literary and artistic criticism can express with reference to each other. The conservative and revolutionary spirit are always wielding drawn daggers. Fundamental distinctions are vehemently maintained as to the very sentiment of beauty, and the application even of the standards of right and wrong to particular cases.

All this is aggravated by the mysterious isolation of each soul. No two men perhaps have ever used precisely the same language, or meant exactly the same thing by identical words. What are grammars, dictionaries, and manuals of different tongues but well-meant attempts to bring about a mere make-belief of unity? No two persons have precisely the same idea about themselves or God, about the world or the universe. Men abreast of each other in science, in philology, in criticism and historical knowledge, fiercely and contemptuously contend against conclusions at which they have severally arrived. Doubtless, master minds which have a certain magnetic power of enforcing their own ideas upon others produce some approximations to unity, but they are lame and halting. Parliaments, senates, universities, brotherhoods, reveal notable but disheartening endeavours after a unity of dissevered souls.

Even religion itself, which ought to blend dissimilar natures in the fervour of common emotions, has been less successful than so-called civilization. The heathen religions are as numerous as the types of character which race and environment have generated. That which is God to one race is often devil to another. That special nation which was trained for two thousand years to bring the world to understand the unity and glory of God broke into fragments, while internal tendencies vehemently opposed each other. Hinduism, Buddhism, and Mohammedanism have been professed by men who fiercely contested within their own pale the most fundamental principles of their respective faiths.

What shall we say of Christianity in this respect? Apart from the deadly animosity which it quickened in the breasts of its enemies, how cruel have been the conflicts between its rival schools! Doubtless there have been moments when Christians were and are still seen to love one another; but a heathen historian bluntly asserts that the rivalry and mutual hostility of Christians is positively more malicious than that of wild beasts. The manner in which the Arian, Nestorian, Monophysite, and Origenistic controversies were conducted is a scandal to humanity. The divisions of Protestantism are obvious consequences of the despotic claims of the Papacy, and hostile sections have used weapons sharpened and poisoned in the armouries of theological and ecclesiastical rivalry in order to abase each other. The efforts to produce and enforce unanimous judgments have in every region absolutely and signally failed.

Nevertheless, He who knew what was in man, while suffering in the furnace of volcanic and titanic antagonisms, and on a site where Eastern and Western cultures were coming into disruptive contact, where Roman and Oriental civilization were fighting no phantom battle, on the night when His perfect goodness had roused the deadliest malice of those who for centuries had been prepared by God's providence to receive their King, but who were actually plotting "the deep damnation" of His judicial murder, prayed to His Father that all His followers "might be one." A unity among men did then present itself to Him, as an object of a prayer which is "always" heard, as the prophecy of a future which must come to pass.

What was that unity? Of what kind and according to what standard?

Absolute *intellectual* oneness and perfect unanimity of human *judgment* could not have been His meaning. What would such a dream as this require before it could be realized? Surely nothing less, to begin with, than a universal language and identical conditions of thought for all men, a state of things than which nothing could be less thinkable. Unanimity of judgment would mean that the endless differences due to climate, race, food, and ideal of happiness must be all reduced to complete uniformity. All the indefinite force of tradition, of inherited sentiment and taste, must be counteracted. Hindu and Chinaman, Saxon and Negro, Arab and Italian, Scandinavian and Hawaiian must severally lose their idiosyncrasies. A unity which demanded such uniformity would be the practical abolition of humanity. None of the striking individualities of our race could survive. There would be no teachers, no rulers, no guides; no discoverers, no heroes, no masters of thought. All would be necessarily brought up or down to the same dead level. Such a consummation is obviously farther off than ever, and utterly undesirable.

But further, the unity for which the blessed Lord prayed must be independent of the forms of government to which either in Church or State those who believed on Him would submit. Monarchy, aristocracy, democracy were severally ruling the affairs of the world, both politically and religiously, in the first century as much as they are in the nineteenth. The unity must be different in kind from that which partially enshrines itself in these forms. It must bind the despot and the slave, and blend the warring elements of a turbulent republic into one fellowship. The sage and the boor, the patriarch and the child, the prince and the menial, the greatest captain and his humblest thrall must on that supposition submit to the same regimen, or be excluded from the unity. The more the prayer is pondered on such lines as these the more impracticable it becomes, except at the cost of the final martyrdom of man, the loss of individuality, and the ultimate repose and frigid death of all that makes up what we know of man.

Is the prayer, then, a hopeless dream? Can it be heard in any sense? Can we hope for or desire its realization? Does the Lord in the very form of His sublime petition suggest the line along which He confidently hopes and predicts its realization or fulfilment? "That they all may be one; even as Thou, Father, art in Me, and I in Thee."

This very analogy suggests that the oneness was not in external organization, not in the rules of some ingeniously compounded society, not in some uniform style of self-manifestation, but "as Thou, Father, art in Me, and I in Thee." Now the burden of much of our Lord's teaching was, "No man hath seen God at any time"—"Ye have neither heard His voice, nor seen His shape." But on the other hand, Jesus Christ was visible, audible, present to men. His face, image, voice, word, life, and example constitute the most potent fact among the grandest that have been achieved in the history of the world.

The union between the Father and Son was the positive antithesis of a union produced by external forms, machinery, or organization. It was absolute but not visible, a mutual indwelling, a spiritual, not formal unity. This simple fact must put us on our guard, when to this, that, or the other organization men point and say that in such a society is the union among believers which answers to the Redeemer's prayer. The very uniformity provokes suspicion. The material completeness and conspicuous visibility of the so-called unity show that it fundamentally violates the analogy which cheered the dying soul of Jesus.

The unity for which He prayed could not be for a fundamental resemblance in self-manifestation; seeing that it was to be as "'Thou, Father, art in Me, and I in Thee,' I pray that they may be one, 'even as We are one.'" The manifestation of the Father differs from the manifestation of the Christ. The infinite Father manifests Himself in all the universe, in every thrill of force, in every star-glint and every atom, in the orbits of planets and the fertilization of mosses, in the pomp of worlds and the sound of many waters; but the manifestation of the *God-Man* is in man— in the tears of penitents and in the consecration of saints, in the enthusiasm and sometimes the clash of opposing interests, in the chastisement and exhaustion of human pride, in the agonies, strong crying, and tears of holy sorrow, in beatitudes and submission, in the faith, courage, and death of martyrs, in the visions and consciousness of the Divine life.

The unity between the Father and the Son was a mutual indwelling—"I in Thee, Thou in Me:" a union of two correlates with each other. All the self-manifestation of the Father culminated in the life of the Son of God. Jesus Christ, "the same yesterday, to-day, and for ever," pours a flood of light upon all the boundless government of the Father, is the type and measure of the pulsations of the heart of Eternal God.

Again, to our limited observation, the whole method of the government of man by the law of God's natural operation takes no account of ignorance, temptation, or fear; it chastises and punishes, and even destroys for the smallest infraction of law, known or unknown. In the course of long lives, in the career of nations and races, we see on which side the Author of Nature stands in man's terrible collision with Him. Only in the Incarnate Word do we learn the law of pardon, regeneration, deliverance from sin, and victory over the world. The cry of the sacrificial Christ is, on behalf of His murderers, "Father, forgive them, for they know not what they do." In the cross of Christ such a revelation is given of the mind of God, and the future life, and of the ends of discipline and death, that the dark side of nature is illumined by a new light. We become reconciled to the Absolute and the Infinite, to the actual supremacy of Divine order, on the one hand; and, on the other, we find that the heart of Jesus is sustained by 'all power that is in heaven and earth." He who has taken our nature into His own is in the Father and the Father in Him.

> "The voice that rolls the stars along
> Speaks all the promises."

Consequently it was not in the *method* and *form* of the self-manifestation of the Father and the Christ, but in the essence of their mutual love, that we see the law of the Divine unity.

The beloved apostle saw in the Lord Jesus when He poured water into the basin to wash His disciples' feet, and never more than then, that He had come out from God and was going back to God, and that the Father had put all things into His hands. The Father then was in Him and He in the Father; the union was certain and eternal, and has never been broken. It is still absolutely perfect, and is a union of essence, of power, of purpose, and of infinite issues to man and to the universe.

Into this union, not of logical formulæ, nor even of modes of manifestation, nor external organization, nor national or ecclesiastical government, the Lord prayed that all that believed in Him should come. The so-called unity of Christendom to be effected by mutual concessions touching the eternal procession of the Spirit, by the terms of some theological formula, by the recognition of this, that, or the other bishop to the highest rank in some indivisible society, even if achieved, might be at once characterized by civil internecine war on other matters arising out of the persistent individualities of men or the idiosyncrasies of nations, and would be in itself, even if successfully performed, a very small and faint adumbration of the real union of the Divine life in the Father and Son.

The union of souls in the common participation of the Divine love is the only perfect union that has ever been achieved among men. This Divine life of the Father and the Son is the same everywhere, in all ages, and in all circumstances. It can transcend and does overleap the barriers of language, of nation, and colour. The persecutor and his victim, the lord and his vassal, the Catholic and the Puritan, the stern iconoclast and the pious pilgrim, whatever may have been his shibboleth, his password, or his pride of birth or station, has felt in the common life of the Spirit his oneness with the Father and the Son. When Huss was on the way to the stake, and saw the enthusiastic votary of the Catholic creed who was bringing a faggot to add to the flame which was to consume him, he is reported to have said, "O sancta simplicitas!" Those two were at that moment truly one in the love that was infinitely above them both. The outcome of the Divine life in man, of the supernatural and new relation to the Father by the Holy Spirit, *is a veritable brotherhood*. Whether this brotherly relation is discovered or not, it is the fundamental reality. It is always waiting for recognition, and transcends and outlives all artificially constructed societies.

The identical results which follow the activity of grace

in human hearts and lives constitute the supreme manifestation of the undivided and indivisible body of the Christ. These results convince the world that He, the Lord and Head of men, the everlasting Son of the Father, has really taken hold of and manifested Himself in the flesh. These glorious *Gesta Christi*, and these alone, harmoniously sing the chorus of thanksgiving to Him that sitteth on the throne, and to the Lamb, for ever and ever.

THE POWERS OF HOLY LOVE.

THE POWERS OF HOLY LOVE.

"The greatest of these is love."—1 COR. xiii. 13.

NUMEROUS attempts have been made to prove that, in some of its aspects, "*love*" is greater than either "faith" or "hope." Some, by narrowing the content of faith to its lowest connotation, by reducing it to intellectual assent, by depriving it of its closely associated graces, and by ridding it of all part in its own glorious issues, have found it an easy task to say that love is greater than faith. Ends are greater than means to the end. The superstructure of a building is nobler than the foundation. The fruit is more than the seed, and so love is obviously greater than faith, as being the end, the fruit, the outcome and upshot of a genuine faith. Now, faith is a right royal gift of God. It is the capacity for blessedness, it is the principle of union with unseen realities, it is the hand which takes hold of the strength of Almighty God. Faith gives validity to promise, and is the only rational treatment that man can offer to truth. What can we do with a truth of any kind except believe in it? It is most certain that by faith we can remove mountains of difficulty, we may overcome the world, we may cast out the devil, and become vividly conscious of the things that are unseen and eternal. "Without faith it is impossible to please God," and "to faith all things are possible," and nothing impossible. Yet in this mighty dithyramb of holy love, we are distinctly told that "now abideth faith, hope, and love, but the greatest of these is love."

Other writers, jealous for the consistency, if not the orthodoxy, of the apostle, have justified this somewhat paradoxical statement by referring to the *perpetuity* of love, as compared with the variableness of faith, and with the temporary aspects and changing qualities of hope. They have quoted St. Paul, when he contrasts the persistence of love with the fleeting phases of prophecy, of great gifts, and of human knowledge; and, contrary to his own statement, have argued that faith will no longer be needed when knowledge and vision have taken its place; that hope will be discarded as useless when we, who now see in a glass darkly, turn round to behold God face to face. "What a man seeth why doth he yet hope for?" Therefore, they argue, love, which is only enhanced by vision, must be greater than faith or hope.

I cannot think that this is the explanation of St. Paul's burning words, "The greatest of these is love." For if we understand anything about the nature of "faith" or "hope," we cannot conceive that they will ever cease to be practical and mighty energies in our spirit-life. Higher faculties than we now possess will but reveal fresh marvels, mysteries, difficulties, and problems to the faculty of faith. Hope, too, will never be exhausted. Every fruition of previously anticipated privilege will wing the flight of fresh expectation and desire. The compass and depth of the Divine fulness are immeasurable and infinite. Besides, the apostle distinctly declares, "Now *abideth* faith, hope, love"—the first and second, as well as the crowning grace,—"these three (*abide*), but the greatest of these is love."

We may, however, take heart for the solution of this paradox, by remembering that "love" is of the very nature of God Himself, that love is His essence, that God is love, and since only by the extravagance and crudity of anthropomorphism could we attribute "faith" or "hope" to God, therefore it is that love is greater than faith, and that love is greater than hope. Since faith and hope imply imperfection of power and state, incompleteness of being, they cannot be equated with the essential glory and greatness of the Divine essence. Love is of God, and it is the peculiarity of this manifestation of the eternal glory, that it demands response of the same kind. We love because He first loved. In the response of love to love, there is the consciousness of our heavenly birth: we discover the Fatherhood; there dawns upon us the sublime and marvellous assurance that we, too, have come from Him, and are returning to Him; that He is ours, and we are His.

There are some who solve the problem of the text by comparing faith in *God* with the love of *man*, to the fearful disparagement of the former. But surely there is no true love of man which does not spring from love of God, and there is no love of God which is not rooted in faith; so that such hurtful comparison or antithesis between "faith" and "love" vanishes into thin air. The comparison on which the depreciatory judgment on faith turns is often enhanced by taking faith as a mere verbal assent to orthodox propositions, thus reducing it to its lowest terms, and taking love in the amplitude of its response to God Himself and then towards all the objects of the Divine love. This leads me to ask your examination of some of the powers or functions of holy love. Love does wonders for faith and hope, and also for knowledge and obedience, transforming the lower forms of these graces into the higher and nobler forms, in an ever-augmenting energy. The deepest, truest love is never satisfied with less than LOVE itself in return, and a love which differs not in kind, though it may in degree. Like the action of the physical heart, it is a perpetual giving and receiving, a reception with no other purpose than to give, a giving with an untiring confidence of a continuous reception. Love is the blending of two natures into one personality. The link between them is so perfect, that each becomes one with the other.

The consequence of these well-known facts is such that, when we speak of "holy love," or "the love of God," we are conscious of what may be called a glorious ambiguity. No logical or grammatical rule can decide apart from context, whether we mean by "love of God" His love to us or our love to Him, or mean by the "love of Christ" His love to us or ours to Him. In the language of the New Testament, the love of God is a divine state, into which His children are brought by the Holy Spirit, and in which there is the fullest, sweetest interchange of holy affection, where the strongest passion is enlisted on the side of the highest principle, and in which the lovers of God love all that He loves with a Divine self-forgetfulness.

It is more easy to write and speculate about "the love of God," and the transformation it can effect in us and in the world, than it is to cherish these sublime affections. God is so august, so immeasurably great, so infinitely good and holy, so far above the influences which disturb our vision and distort our conceptions, that we often tremble at our audacity in speaking of the love that prevails between us. Some exposition, however, of the nature and power of love may not be useless. The apparent revolution of a planet round its primary is really explained to our thought by the common revolution of both planet and primary around their common centre of gravity. The earth and the sun alike revolve around a point central to the two. That point is far within the body of the sun. So of every other body in the vast system of which the sun is the centre. The sun as surely revolves round the smallest asteroid as round the vast system of Saturn, and so it holds all these common centres within the mighty embrace of its own being. We obtain hence some notion, some faint illustration of the relation sustained towards Himself by every soul that is born of God. There is a mutual gravitation, and a genuine centre of revolution for God and every soul smitten by the power of holy love. There is twofold attraction, a twofold and mutual self-abandonment of the one to the other. God is as surely and as fully drawn to the soul as the soul is to Him. "Love" in this large sense cannot be limited to one or the other of the subjects of this twofold synthesis. God loves man, man loves God. God is attracted to man, man draws nigh to God. Each loses itself in the other. This state of soul is blessed beyond words. Those who have become fully subject to it can hardly be conscious of it, for it is deeper than consciousness. It is heaven itself, where meditation upon personal blessedness is left far behind and below, and the realization of the Eternal Life takes its place.

We are a long way, here and now, from this perfect accord; for "in us, that is in our flesh, there dwelleth no good thing." In the regenerate there is still the centrifugal passion, which is ever aiming at severance from the highest love, and which would rush into the ghastly darkness of a perfect independence of the Divine love.

Only once has "the Word become flesh," and humanity been utterly interpenetrated with the Divine light, and the issue of this sublime conjunction was that even the flesh of Christ put on immortality, was received up into glory, and is set down on the right hand of the eternal Majesty. Still it is possible for holy love to make continuous advance to the fulness of communion with God. "We have received of His fulness, and grace over against grace," in every augmenting pulse of holy affection in all the sacred interchanges of holy love.

This becomes manifest when we consider the several relations which love sustains to OBEDIENCE, KNOWLEDGE, FAITH, and HOPE. There are several wide and suggestive utterances of Holy Scripture which appear contradictory until we have discovered this fundamental law of holy love. The most obvious contradiction in form is between certain statements of our Lord. Thus He says, on the one hand, "If ye love Me, keep My commandments." In this exhortation, love to Christ is the mighty energy that produces holy obedience. The loving eye is quick to discern the will, the wish of the beloved. The heart which truly loves cannot break one of the least of these commandments. Even if the commandment seem arbitrary, it is enough that He who is supremely loved has said, "This do in remembrance of Me." That is enough. Such motive is sufficient. It is simple, clear, and explicit. The obedience which is the witness, the pledge, the consequence of love, and is neither formal nor perfunctory, but the outcome of a self-sacrificing affection, is alone well-pleasing. This idea pervades the language alike of prophets and apostles. Isaiah and St. Paul combine to repudiate an obedience which springs from any lower motive. Here we find a link which unites the Old Testament with the New. Two great principles emerge as we contemplate it. One is : (1) We must *not* dignify by the name of LOVE that which is unwilling or unable to yield obedience to the beloved, or which is not strong enough to overcome all our carnal reluctance to do that which God commands. (2) We dare not build anything upon an OBEDIENCE which is not the child and the consequence of a genuine love. But is this all? Certainly not. Our Lord says elsewhere, " He that hath My commandments and keepeth them, he it is that loveth Me : and he that loveth Me shall be loved of My Father, and I will love him ;" and again, "If ye keep My commandments, ye shall abide in My love."

At first sight it would seem that "obedience" is regarded in these words as the parent of love, not only the pledge, but the occasion of mutual love, and of all the Divine interchanges of sacred affection; in other words, *that obedience and love had changed places!* It might seem from this exhortation that an authoritative command was jarring with that gracious self-abandonment to which love calls. But is not the solution of the apparent discord found in the following underlying thought? There is verily a love which prompts to obedience, but this obedience, again, is the stimulus and food, the provocative and the ground of a still higher love, leading on to a sublimer response of mutual affection. We begin by "loving little;" but if the little love is strong enough to express itself by keeping the commandments of love, the love grows by what expresses it: and the higher love leads to a more complete obedience, and so on for ever. The burning seraph loves, because he goes and returns (on the Divine behests), "as it were a flash of lightning." Obedience is the libration of the wings of love. Love flames into seraphic fire when fed with the oil of obedience.

The powers of love reveal themselves in like manner in their relation to *knowledge*. Take the text, "This is life eternal, that they might know Thee the only veritable God, and Jesus Christ whom Thou hast sent." The KNOWLEDGE is life eternal. Not to know God is to abide in death and darkness. We read elsewhere that life itself is the light of men. "They that know Thy name will put their trust in Thee," and "Thou wilt keep him in perfect peace whose mind is stayed on Thee, because he trusteth in Thee." All this is re-echoed from every part of Divine Revelation. There is a knowledge, a full assurance, a divine intuition of the living God, which is life eternal. The beatific vision is but the perfection of the knowledge of God. It is the complete satisfaction of our whole spiritual nature: we who pant and yearn after reality, after eternal truth, can only find it in the *knowledge of God*.

Yet there are many things said of *knowledge, per se*, which baffle us. Elsewhere we read that "*knowledge* puffeth up." St. Paul tells us in this chapter that we may have the gifts of knowledge, may understand all mysteries, may speak with the tongues of men and angels, may prophesy with fine intuition of the truth, and yet be mere clanging cymbals, or sounding brass. In order to meet this apparent contradiction, we may remember that without some knowledge, without mental realization of truth, we can put truth to no use. Knowledge, acquaintance with the idea of God, must, by the nature of the case, precede credence and love.

Knowledge is a necessary preliminary to faith and its attendant virtues. How can we believe that which is not made *known* to us? At times, moreover, knowledge in its deepest sense and most life-giving essence is shown to be dependent on putting into practice, on *doing* that which we *know* to be right, by not only "hearing," but "doing" the sayings of Christ. At other times we are told that obedience, a willingness to do the will of God, will open the eyes of the understanding to appreciate, to *know* the doctrine, whether it be of God. At other times "knowledge" is boldly contrasted with love. "Knowledge puffeth up," "Love buildeth up;" while knowledge without love is nothing worth. So that knowledge is at one time represented as an essential preliminary to both faith and obedience; and, again, at other times, knowledge is represented as even dependent upon and actually conditionated by a heartfelt obedience.

What we have already seen to be the value and place of holy obedience may help us to resolve this seeming contradiction; but we have more certain and satisfying light upon this mystery in the profound utterance of St. John: "He that loveth not, knoweth not God." This is true of other objects, both of love and knowledge, as certainly as it is true of the love and knowledge of the Lord God. We do not know any thing, any person, any science, until we love it. The "dry light" needed for scientific pursuit is the eye unbleared by prejudice, unfilled with tears of foolish and inappropriate emotion, not an eye which does not flash with love. It is sometimes said that "Love is blind." Cupid has been imaged with shaded eyes. No greater mistake can be made. Love has microscopic eyes to see both the faults and excellences of the beloved object. What a world this would be if mothers could see in all children the divine attractions and worth which they do see in their firstborn; and if lovers could see in all persons the wonderful lovableness they easily discern in one another! It is only the LOVER of truths, of persons, of countries, of great causes and principles, who really and veritably knows them. He that loveth not his country, does not know it. He that loveth not Nature, does not know it. He that is not ready to sacrifice his own pleasure to secure the triumph of a great principle, does not know that principle. I do not mean that he shows himself to be ignorant of it, seeing that, if he knew it better, he would love it more; but that the love, the going out of self towards an object, is itself revelatory of the object. Consequently, and *à fortiori, he that loveth not God, knoweth not God.* Love is actually the condition of the highest knowledge. If this be a law of knowledge, then we see at once how easy it is to explain the relations of knowledge and life, and of knowledge and obedience, which puzzled us just now.

The difficulty is resolved thus:—There is a kind of knowledge which is a necessary antecedent to any faith, to any obedience, to any love; and yet such knowledge may remain barren and useless for the higher life. We may, as many do, know, and fall short of believing; know, and not obey; know, and refuse to love. Such knowledge may puff up its possessor and vaunt itself. It leads nowhither, it is neither life nor peace. But there is another knowledge, born of simple obedience and holy love, and this knowledge is "life eternal." So we gather from this meditation another of the powers of "holy love." It transforms the incipient knowledge, the verbal assent to propositions, into the invincible assent of full assurance. The knowledge of the only true God and Jesus Christ which is born of holy love, quickened and stimulated by the microscopic eye of strong, reverent affection, is nothing short of the beatific vision; it is, as our Lord said, *life eternal.*

In close relation, and by similarity of argument, we see that other powers of holy love give great intensity to *faith* and *hope.*

There are degrees of *faith,* varying from simple credence, admission of the truth of certain facts without passion or any corresponding conduct, on to a certainty which tends to high and appropriate emotions, to the full assurance which appeals to and absorbs the whole nature. Faith varies from the admission of a moderate probability to the vision and revelation of the Lord. The degrees of faith differ, as a solitary grain of mustard-seed differs from the vast forest-tree trembling at every point with the wealth and glory of its developed life. What is the energy by which faith passes from stage to stage? Faith is energetic through *love.* Divinely implanted love, spiritually inspired self-surrender increases every faculty of knowledge, deepens every impression made by truth, opens the eye which indifference or passion had blinded, purifies the gaze which prejudice or evil bias had corrupted and obscured, and so makes the trembling faith which can only cry, "I believe, help my unbelief," grow, burn, gleam with holy enthusiasm, until it cries, "I know whom I have believed, and I am persuaded."

There is faith which leads to love and is manifested in

love, but there is the higher faith which is born of a perfect trust, and which again in its turn blazes into the flame of that holy confiding love which cries, "I am persuaded that neither death, nor life, nor things present, nor things to come, nor principalities, nor powers, nor height, nor depth, nor any other creature, shall be able to separate me from the love of God which is in Christ Jesus my Lord."

In like manner there are degrees of "*hope.*" Who has not experienced what he and others call Christian hope, but which on close analysis is found to be little better than a faint and feeble desire after better things, and a desponding cry of the soul for what is just a grade better than blank despair? This is not the hope that saves. Contrast it with the full evidence of things hoped for, which is imparted by living faith. Let desire be large, and expectation strong; let hope embrace all Divine promises, and it becomes a vast capacity for blessedness, and often bursts out in solitary places and on dark nights into songs of rejoicing. Then is revealed what the apostles call "patience," born of quiet waiting, with a smile upon its face, reflecting all the lustre of the Divine manifestation. Tribulation and sorrow are but the crucible in which this precious quality and energy of soul is refined. "This hope maketh not ashamed," and can never be disappointed, because it is a veritable prelibation of its own object—it is the earnest and foretaste of the purchased possession. We ask once more, what leads the soul from hope to hope, from the faint uplifting of the wearied weeping eye to the "hope full of immortality"? St. Paul gives us the answer: "Because the love of God is shed abroad in our hearts by the Holy Spirit given to us."

In this answer, moreover, the apostle throws a flood of

light upon what he meant by "THE LOVE OF GOD," and reminds us that he identified it, here and elsewhere, with the whole of that supernatural and new life which is produced in the spirit of man by the Holy Spirit of God. "Regeneration," "a new creature," "consecration," "sanctification," "resurrection and ascension with Christ" are terms which in part adumbrate the full effect of the baptism with the Holy Ghost, or the indwelling of the Holy Spirit of God in the life of man. Consequently, what in one place St. Paul calls the "fruits of the Spirit," elsewhere he verbally enumerates as the powers of Holy Love. This apparent inconsistency is resolved by perceiving the glorious fact that the Holy Spirit brings the soul into genuine, veritable relations of love to God, and into the spiritual consciousness of the love of God. Thus it is that incipient knowledge, quickened by love, becomes the knowledge born of love, which is life eternal; that faith which trembles on the verge of extinction becomes a faith active through love to remove mountains; that hope becomes the anchor of the soul, sure and steadfast; and that obedience becomes an absolute submission, a self-abandonment, and a beatific vision.

Just as the relations of the soul with God are deepened and enriched by holy love, thus fully justifying the high eulogiums of the apostle, so all our relations with our fellow-men are heightened and sanctified by the love which, at the cross of Christ, we have learned to cherish towards them.

We must know something of men before we love them, but when the souls of men become precious to us in the light of heavenly love, then we begin to know them and their worth, to estimate them at the price set upon them by their Redeemer; finally, as the outcome of such knowledge, the love breaks forth afresh and never faileth. In like manner, our hope for the future of our *race* will, on the basis of God's love, lead to zealous and stimulating effort for the amelioration of the *race;* and such a love reveals the awful and glorious facts of the redemption of the soul and of the *race*. When love has educated our hope it becomes invincible, it towers over the harsh and cold judgments of the world, it anticipates the ultimate victory.

The powers of this holy love turn faith into vision, hope into rapture, effort into triumph, and earth into heaven.

FAITH THE MEASURE OF BLESSING.

Preached on May 28, 1891, in the Cheshunt College Chapel, at the ordination of two students appointed to missionary service, the one in Mongolia, the other in Madagascar.

FAITH THE MEASURE OF BLESSING.

"Great is thy faith: be it done unto thee even as thou wilt."—ST. MATT. xv. 28.

WHILE faith occupies a most conspicuous place in the New Testament, as the instrument by which men become united to God, and are prepared and qualified to receive the light and peace of the gospel, we must be upon our guard against drawing too much conclusion from the analogical lessons of our Lord's miracles. The method of Divine mercy varies in each case. When Christ called Matthew from the receipt of custom, the imperative summons was immediately obeyed. When our Lord, in the royalty of His love, spake to the dull, cold ear of death, there is no hint that the child of the centurion, or that the widow's son, or that the spirit of Lazarus was stirred into faith by the person or claims of Jesus. In these and other instances, Christ declared Himself independent of any human condition whatever on the part of the recipient, yet, in a multitude of other cases, He did regard faith, moral surrender to His will, profound recognition of His claims as the channel of His noblest gifts, and as the measure of the kind and degree of blessing which He was able to impart. "Believe ye that I am able to do this?" is the question he put to the blind men of Bethsaida. "If thou canst do anything," is the language of the father of the epileptic child. In our Lord's reply, He seemed to reproach the half-faith which made so feeble a draft upon the almightiness of God, and cried, "If thou canst believe, . . . all things are possible." He could not do many mighty works, because of the unbelief of His own people.

Here the Lord makes the faith of a heathen woman the measure of the blessing she might draw forth from His Divine power. Faith in the nature and promises of God's greatest self-manifestation appears the normal method for the bestowment of Divine blessing. Faith on sufficient evidence, moral acquiescence in the character and claims of the living Christ, is the prime condition of life itself. Faith is the capacity for blessedness and the condition of power. It is the eye by which we see supernal beauty, the hand with which we grasp exhaustless treasure, the ear into which falls the melody and harmony of truth, the faculty for tasting the sweetness of the Divine mercy, of acquiescing in the mastery and supremacy of the Divine will, and the power by which we take hold of God and abandon self to the ends of the kingdom of God.

Now, I have chosen the words of my text, as graciously uttered by the Lord Himself to you and other young servants of Christ on the eve of departure to the work of foreign missions. There are many analogies between your yearnings and passionate pleading and those of the Syrophenician woman. The narratives contained in the Gospels of Matthew and Mark describe the approach of the blessed Lord to the confines of the heathen world. He seems to have gone into the coasts of Tyre and Sidon to prove to His disciples that His gospel broke through the narrow boundaries within which both Pharisees and Sadducees would confine any Messianic privileges. He had no sooner come into the borders of heathendom, than some presented themselves who had apparently a vague knowledge of His claims and powers, and who began to draw at once upon His resources. A mother's heart pleaded wildly, importunately for her child that was grievously vexed with a devil. The disciples were impatient. "Send her away," said they, "for she crieth after us." For a moment, Christ seemed as if He were deaf to her importunity, and were yielding to the Pharisaic prejudices of His own disciples: "He answered never a word." Again came the moan, "O Lord, Thou Son of David, have mercy." Then, as though He would express and so condemn the Judaic withholding of grace from heathendom, and as if He would expose the pride which was ready to burst from the lips of His disciples, He said, "I was not sent but unto the lost sheep of the house of Israel." Thus He put the mother's heart to a still severer strain, and she fell at His feet and worshipped Him, saying, "Lord, help me." Then once again reiterating in stronger language the universal feeling of the Pharisees and Sadducees, He said, "It is not meet to take the children's bread and cast it to the dogs." One's heart quails to hear from the lips of the Saviour these terrible repulses of the heathen woman's plea. Her pertinacity and enthusiasm see through the apparent harshness of His words; she must have perceived some deeper reason for them, and some meaning of His apparently haughty rejoinder, as she crouched before Him, and cried again, "True, Lord, let the children have their bread; but the little dogs eat of the crumbs which fall from the master's table." The loving heart of Jesus was awaiting that final intercession. He drew it from her broken spirit, and the grand, abundant, lavish gift was dispensed with royal largess, "Great is thy faith: be it done unto thee even as thou wilt."

Much depends upon the voice which utters such approval and promise, whether it be that of the world, or the Church, or of the Lord Himself; but let us think for a moment of the analogies between you and this importunate intercessor. Do you not take upon your heart and upon your lips the necessitous cry of the world that is sitting in darkness and in the shadow of death? Notwithstanding all the wondrous leading of Providence, all the light that lighteneth every man, and all the striving of the Holy Ghost, and though there is much that is good and true in some of the systems of heathen thought, do you not feel that the object of your self-annihilating love, that this heathen world, is "grievously vexed with the devil"? Have you not identified yourself with the suffering and ignorance, the madness of a lost soul, so as to plead concerning it, "Have mercy upon me"? Do not the scorn and prejudice, the spirit of aristocratic monopoly falling from the lips of modern Pharisee and Sadducee, verily burn into your soul when they seem to your troubled heart to be sanctioned by the coldness of the Church and the silence of the Lord? Do not the methods which He uses to test your courage and to rebuke His half-hearted disciples pierce you to the quick? And when the voice comes which apparently implies that the Bread of Life, the gospel of Divine love, is only meant for English folk, and that Fetichism is good enough for New Guinea, and Confucius all-sufficient for

China,—that it is not meet to take the children's bread and cast it to the dogs,—are you not smitten to your knees? But, my brethren, you are not repulsed even by that supposition, for you know that there is bread enough and to spare; that even the crumbs from the Master's table may, in the Master's hands, be multiplied so as to fill all mouths, and satisfy all needs. You know that there is "enough for each, for all, for evermore" at the table of the Lord, and you boldly face the facts and the apparent impossibilities that even grace should ever overtake these millions of starving men. At length the Lord, who knows all that you feel, lets fall upon your yearning heart the words, "Great is thy faith; be it done unto thee even as thou wilt." Yet, before I ask you to accept this lifegiving assurance that your faith is the measure and the prophecy, and even the channel of Divine benediction, I must remind you that THE WORLD tells you, with cynical and ironical compliment, that your *faith* is indeed "great." You hear the tones of its scornful laughter rippling through the popular journals, "Great is thy faith!" What is meant, however, by the world's ironical compliment is little more than a heartless reproach, for, in other words, it declares that you have yielded to some spasm of excited feeling, that you have been stirred by some imperfect apprehension of your task, that you are going to take part in a solemn farce, that you are going on a fool's errand. Your faith has run away with your prudence, your glowing motives transcend your reason. "Great" indeed is your faith if you imagine that you can sap the giant upas-tree of caste in India, or grapple with the ancient superstitions of Feng-shui in China, or present a doctrine which will be more acceptable to Mandarins than the ethics or history or minstrelsy of their sacred books. "'Great,'" says the jesting world, "'is your faith' if you think that you can prove that 'the Light of the world' shines more brilliantly than 'the light of Asia.' 'Great is your faith' if you believe that with your schools or with the veneer of Western civilization drawn over the untamed passions of the Malagasy, or the Papuan, you will ultimately transform them into Christian people. Atheism, Pantheism, and Fetichism, idolatry and caste, opium and alcohol, slavery and lust will be too mighty for you. 'Great is your faith'!" Meanwhile, you, brethren, bear up bravely under this avalanche of reproach, and you are confident that a faith which scattered the Olympian gods from their high places in Europe, which has abolished the most loathsome and cruel barbarism by the magic of its revelations, which has secured its trophies in every field of exertion, and over every kind of man, *may*, even in your hands, do wonders yet again. You have each taken upon your heart the burden of a world, you have agonized over its sorrows and have identified yourselves with the sufferers, and you confidently appeal to the Lord for mercy. I hear you murmuring day and night in your prayers to God, "Lord, help me; Lord, help me! This heathen world, for which I am willing to give my life, is grievously vexed and ready to die."

But the CHURCH itself—English society, indeed, in its multiform aspects and activities—often smiles its approval at the enthusiasm which is burning up your self-will and consecrating your life. The approval does not always amount to sympathy. The Church at home, though it has supplied the sinews of war, and a machinery which positively is on a large scale, utterly fails as yet to appreciate the magnitude of the task before it. When, like the woman of our narrative, the missionary's eager cry falls on the ear of the disciples, we hear some sensible and devout persons echo the cold rejoinder, "'Send her away, for she crieth after us.' We have too much to do at home to attend to this importunate appeal." Even the Church misapprehends the test to which the Lord submits it, when He seems, for our rebuke, to let us have our selfish way, and suppose that we are the only sheep of His pasture, that we *must* have our privileges, our attractive services, our powerful preachers, our sacred music, our treats and comforts, the banquet in the Father's house, let the slaves and the dogs, the lepers and the pariahs of the world, the fanatical Hindu, the self-satisfied Moslem fare as they may. When the Lord, to our confusion, sends us a plentiful feast, but sends leanness into our souls, missionaries are fain, nay, are compelled to plead for the crumbs, the fragments, the broken pieces for the dying world, which is still grievously vexed by the devil and all his angels. But, my beloved young friends, take no rebuff. Plead on with God and with men. Be true princes with God in the strife, and overcome Omnipotence with your cry. Let us, under the glances of our Lord's criticizing love, see what the rich man's table is. How it groans with delicacies, and is garnished with all kinds of savoury viands! how often the voice is heard, "The oxen and fatlings are ready, the corn and wine and oil are served, all things are ready!" At length, after many delays and excuses, the banquet is furnished with guests; the song and enthusiasm rise high. *Te Deums* and *Magnificats* are chanted in joyful chorus; waste of strong emotion occurs, and fruitless shouts of triumph simply end in desire for another banquet, as rich in provision, and as finely seasoned with minstrelsy. On such occasions you say to one another, "Oh for the crumbs which fall from the rich man's table!" What would the heathen world not give for service which, however faithful and spiritual, is not seasoned up to the fastidiousness of modern English taste? If heathendom were at liberty to feed on the fragments that remain over and above when all the invited guests are satisfied, there would be enough and to spare. So, my dear young brethren, pause not in your pleading for help, and call upon the Lord. Give Him no peace until He arise and have mercy, and then most assuredly the voice will come from His excellent glory— "Young men, great is your faith; be it done unto you even as you will."

When St. Peter in the direst extremity cried aloud, "Lord, save *me!*" he was thinking only of his own life; and the Lord's answer was, "O thou of *little* faith, wherefore didst thou doubt?" but when the Syrophenician woman had lost herself in the safety of her child, and, against all temptation to distrust, and even to hopelessness, had not yet despaired of the love or power of the Son of man, He read the depths of that riven heart, and said, "O woman, *great* is thy faith!" Thus the faith of an apostle in those days may have been less than the faith of a youth in these days who, looking the black darkness of devil-ridden masses in the face, is persuaded that Christ is able and willing "to save to the uttermost all that come unto God by Him." But let us observe that a "*little* faith" may grow to more, may perceive in the very silence and reserve, and even in the repulses of the blessed Lord, new phases of His nature, and may cherish fresh love to His person, and so the ground of confidence in Him may increase, until it becomes "*great.*" Faith neither seeks nor finds a demonstration that the mind cannot resist. It may be so when He comes in the clouds and every eye shall see Him; but as yet a veil is round about His throne. You do not pretend to have received an absolute or final revelation, but such is your confidence in that which you have received, that the Lord responds to your self-consecration, "Great is your faith."

Knowledge, love, faith, prayer, service,—what strange powers they possess! They are linked with each other as heat, motion, electricity, light are related to each other, and they have a tendency to produce one another. There must be some initial knowledge to believe and to love; but just in proportion to the simplicity of your faith and the reality of your love is your knowledge deepened. When this higher knowledge breaks upon you, then your faith becomes a full assurance, an invincible and real assent; then love burns more fervently and flashes a higher enthusiasm for holy service, and demands self-abandonment. If faith be great and strong, it becomes a *prophecy*, a seeing of the invisible, a knowledge of what the will of the Lord is. Your hand takes hold of the Lord's hand; His strength is made perfect in your weakness. The expression of your faith is twofold. It takes the form of prayer and service, of intercourse with God and consecrated life. The highest conception of prayer is revealed to us in the intercession of Jesus. Some have told us that the prayers of Jesus are a positive disproof of the idea of the God-Man. How, say they, should God in Christ pray to God? My brethren, it seems to me that only in the God-Man, in the incarnation of eternal wisdom and power and love in Jesus, can the function of prayer be fully exercised, and only here do we see its true ideal realized. Only He could say, "I know that Thou hearest Me always." His perfect harmony with the will of God rendered His prayer a prediction of what would be. His desires, for ever weaving themselves into supplications, or rather communings with the central and supreme Power of the universe, became the programme of Providence and the outline of the future. Further, it is just in proportion as your own hearts and minds rise up into the heart and will of your Lord, that *your* importunate prayer also becomes a prophecy of God's ways, an anticipation of what *He* will do. You are let into the secret of His heart; you know that the answer of love is near, and that the Lord Jesus will triumph. There is no apparent limit to His grace. Ask what you will, and it shall be given; seek what you intensely desire, since He gave you the desire, and you shall find. Press Him hard with what faith tells you is veritably in harmony with His will, and you will have the answer of peace. Certainly, if God hears the prayer of man at all, either the wishes of man prevail over the decrees of God, or the desires of man must have been purified and lifted up into the purposes of the Eternal. But this is not the whole of the mystery and miracle of prayer. The prayers, the desires, of men are part at least of the ways in which these purposes of God are effectuated. God would seem to have declared Himself incapable of feeding one of His creatures by bread only. He must give desire or hunger as well as food. He must give not only the wondrously constructed atmosphere, but the power to breathe it. There is no calculation of the extent to which the yearning of any one of us may not bring down blessings upon ourselves and upon one another. Unutterably close, but for the most part unconscious, is the interwining of human destinies. Pray, then, without ceasing, and your prayer may be not only the sign of your having entered into the heart of God, but the very channel by which the prayer will be answered. Your faith is great. Be it unto you according as you will.

Count upon great things; go to heathen lands with large desires that the evil may be exorcised. Count upon much blessing for these lands that need so much grace, for these souls that are bound and manacled, not with feeble threads, but with fetters of iron. If your faith is great, your cry will be importunate and triumphant, and your life will correspond with your faith.

You may ask me, What faith are you suggesting? Is it simply faith in a Divine call to this work, and a persuasion that God is good, infinitely better than we are, to these heathen peoples? To my mind it is more than this. I admit that no great thing has often (perhaps ever) been done in this world, save by those who *were*, and who felt that they were, *predestined* by God to serve Him along certain revealed lines. Think of Abraham and Moses, David and St. Paul, St. Athanasius and St. Augustine, Luther and Columbus, Cromwell and Livingstone. These men believed that God had destined them for their special services; but the faith of which these and many other narratives speak is a faith about and in God. It is a saturation of mind with, and submission of the whole will to, a great revelation of the righteousness and mercy of God proclaimed in the atoning work, in the Divine majesty and claims of Jesus Christ, and in the healing power of the Spirit of the Lord Jesus.

Faith is often charged with being credulity of understanding, acceptance of statements from teachers without sufficient evidence or reason. The charge ignores the fact that we possess a religious nature and sensibility which sees the invisible, and which gives invincible assurance; and that the highest truths and realities thus cognized are more certain to those who apprehend them than any conclusions drawn from sensible phenomena or one-sided logic. Faith is often confounded with vain religiosity, as though the *facts* presented to the moral and religious faculties were not as reliable as those which are offered to the senses of men and generalized by the experts of science. Those thinkers and workers will rule the future who stand closest to *all* the facts; certainly, not those who ignore the chief facts revealed to our religious nature, and facts, moreover, which are the key of knowledge to all the facts and mysteries of the universe.

Faith is not compatible with the self-sufficient repudiation of the voice that has come to you from the excellent glory, nor is it a blind passion to diffuse some speculation of your own; neither is it a vague belief that it will be all right, or all the same with everybody. If you have no steadfast conviction, no real message, no abiding objective fact which stirs, goads, forces you from within to obey its behests, it is not too late to renounce the enterprise. Great faith in ample and sufficient power to meet every kind of sickness and peril of our humanity will secure the Divine response, and this it is which we covet, for you and for ourselves, "Be it unto you according as you will." My brethren, what is it that you will for the heathen world? Is it simply the blessing of Western civilization, the introduction of a higher education, the uprising of a noble discontent, the careful formulation of a logical creed, the founding of new institutions? Verily, all these things are good as means to an end; but nothing short of that end can satisfy you, and the end itself is what you have so far entered into the heart of Jesus as to crave, and into the purpose and work of the Christ as to desire beyond all other things.

Now, no such prayer as this is rational without corresponding effort, and such conduct and consecration of life as may conduce to the sublime end of all this soul-hunger. A self-indulgent life would vitiate the prayer for help. Self-consideration, collision with God, rebellion against His providence or against the disappointments of your service, or any weariness or resentment at the apparent silence of God our Lord, will eat out the spirit and power of prayer. There does come at times over the spirit of every missionary a feeling of hopelessness, as though he had attempted more than was rational or even possible; but do not exaggerate this sentiment, because, here at home, and indeed in all departments of service, we are attempting absolute impossibilities unless we know how to make use of Divine power. What can the electrician or engineer, the astronomer or the navigator accomplish, until he finds out the use of the inexhaustible energies of Nature, or rather of the Author of Nature? What can the Christian do, in facing the tremendous mysteries of life and death, but find out how to appropriate infinite power, righteousness, and love? We here, you there, are attempting impossibilities to the mere wisdom or power of man: but the truths you have to speak are seeds; the seed of the great Harvest is the Word of God. The light of the Sun of Righteousness is shining in the darkest lands. The head waters of the river of life are ready to diffuse themselves. Think well what it is, then, that you "*will*" for heathendom, and it shall be done. While you go forth on this great enterprise, many will follow you with their prayers, and, "like a fountain, day and night," will rise the cry of fellow-feeling, of deepest sympathy, and continual intercession for you to the heart of Jesus, to the throne of God.

THE FULNESS OF THE BLESSING OF THE CHRIST.

Preached on June 3, 1891, at Robertson Street Chapel, Hastings, at the ordination of a missionary appointed for service in New Guinea.

THE FULNESS OF THE BLESSING OF THE CHRIST.

"When I come unto you, I shall come in the fulness of the blessing of the Christ."—ROM. xv. 29.

A MIST hangs over the future of our earthly life, as impenetrable as that which conceals the invisible world. The possibilities, perils, temptations, and tasks of the future, the collapse of our brightest anticipations, the development of unknown powers now slumbering within us, the utter change of our surroundings, the possible assaults upon our character, the cruelty of the world, the triumphs of grace, may lead us through greater mysteries than the valley of the shadow of death itself. The petulant coward who takes his own life confesses that it is easier to face the invisible and eternal world than to encounter the reproach of men or the difficulties of circumstance. The martyr can rush to the stake rather than condescend to tamper with conscience or be treacherous to truth, and he confesses that the mystery of human life on earth is as great as the mystery of eternity.

Every man who has an unknown enterprise before him

observes, it is true, a line of light borrowed from his own or his brother's scant experience which indicates the probable form of his earthly future, but as to the perplexing and all-important details of time and season, of success or failure, of bereavement or privation, he knows nothing, he sees through a glass darkly. The young missionary who forms only the faintest image of the principalities and powers that will confront him, who anticipates poignantly the peril arising from the hypocrisy or insensibility of the heathen, the agony which creeps over him from the ennui and isolation of his own heart or the gigantic work he is attempting, may rationally feel that he has undertaken a responsibility utterly beyond his own strength. My young brother, unless you are sent forth by Christ Himself, the difficulties which encumber and encompass you will be too great for you. You need the sense of alliance with supernatural order and of Divine commission, and you must be as sure as St. Paul was of your moral union with Christ, you must be certified that nothing can separate you from the love of God which is in Christ Jesus. You must be sure of yourself to this extent, that, whatever happens to you, Christ is the same, and your moral relation to Him cannot be essentially modified in any conceivable circumstance that may arise, either in this world or the next world. St. Paul ultimately reached Rome in a different plight from that which he anticipated when he wrote these exhilarating words, nevertheless they were a true description of the mood, the courage, the hopefulness, the faith, the vision with which he faced the Roman courts, the Prætorian guards, the unbelieving Jews, the Christian believers of the imperial city. Bonds and imprisonment awaited him, but "in the fulness of the blessing of the Christ" he knew how to be abased. Contradiction and blaspheming confronted him, but in the power of that fulness of blessing he learned in whatever state he was, therewith to be content. Dark hours rolled over him, but the fulness of the blessing turned the shadow of death into the morning. Unbelief, ignorance, idolatry and lies, unutterable sins and the memory of his own rebellion against the supreme love harrowed his tender heart, but it was his earnest expectation and burning desire that Christ might be magnified either in his life or by his death. The fulness of the blessing encompassed him like a cloud of glory. When he was weak, then he was strong; he found in it consolation in distress and strength for duty. Let us take the same motto as our breastplate and our helmet, our shield and sword, and thus equip ourselves for every great and solemn undertaking, however mysterious it may be.

There are other and rival principles of service. Many of these are fairly excellent in their way, and need not be discounted as valueless; but, my young brother, they are not adequate to your requirements. (1) Thus the fulness of the blessings of *Western civilization* is not to be underrated. Roads and houses, ships and weapons, tools and books, legitimate trade and applied science are admirable; but you have something more precious than all these. Music and medicine and magic lanterns may arrest attention, but nothing short of the blessing of the Christ will be the panoply in which you move, and the treasure you have to convey. Again: (2) the fulness of the blessing of a *sound and liberal education* is ennobling and uplifting. You must and will endeavour to quicken all the mental faculties of the heathen among whom you live, and will put every healthful thought into the minds of the young generation that is rising around you. But you go in the full determination to lead them into the highest wisdom needed by sage and child, by Greek and Barbarian, bond and free; you would make them wise unto salvation, or you fail altogether. Again: (3) you might go in the fulness of the blessing of an *orthodox creed;* and few are less ready than I to undervalue the vast importance of a sound and rational construction of Christian belief. A thinker who has no theological principles, and no settled convictions which link him with the great brotherhood of believers,—who has no tidings, no message to deliver which he holds to be true and trustworthy,—is exposed to confusion at the blast of the hostile wind of controversy or doctrine. But you are in dire need of what is incalculably more precious still, viz. the fulness of the blessing of the living Christ. (4) You might go in the fulness of the blessing of an *ordination* granted to you by Episcopal hands, linking you by some artificial mechanism with the historic Churches of England or Rome. I am far from denying that some men may find this to be a comfort, an inspiration, and a strength to them. They may assert, and the heathen may believe, that they, in virtue of this, can work invisible and impalpable miracles upon the bodies and souls of men. But *you* need that which is indefinitely greater than this; you, if you go, must do so in the fulness of the blessing of the ever-living and Divine Christ Himself. Without the realization of that supreme benediction, which is more real than any other fact in your experience, not only you, but they also, will utterly fail of the end at which you both aim. (5) Some, again, go forth in what they regard as the fulness of the blessing of some critical methods, or of certain scientific dogmas, which happen to be in vogue to-day, but which will be strangely modified to-morrow, which need a power of criticism yet before they are verified, and often lead honest men into perilous confusion before they are aware. Weapons of distinction and precision are very well in their way, but they recoil on those who use them carelessly or ignorantly. The knowledge of them ofttimes puffeth up, and recklessly destroys that which should be tenderly protected from injury. You cannot do without the fulness of a blessing which, being already verified in your own experience, is above all suspicion and proof against all criticism, one which you invincibly hold, as a reality more certain than any dogma, however it is bepraised or trusted. (6) Some missionaries may enter on their work in the fulness of the blessing of a vigorous *philanthropy*, of a doctrine of ascetic self-sacrifice, of a manly determination to live a good life before men, doing justly and loving mercy, setting forth an example of fortitude and charity, purity and justice. Nor do I assert that such purposes are vain or fruitless. Beautiful buildings may be raised upon sand, or constructed upon ice; but rain and wind and even sunshine will level them to the ground. Principles like these need a deep foundation or a living root. Graces of character which have no spiritual source resemble artificial flowers surreptitiously threaded to a barren or dead tree. You crave some stronger principle, some surer benediction, and you will not find this except in the real presence of Him who is the life-giving source of all holiness, and in the constraining energy of a love to Him who is the Life and Light of the world, " Jesus Christ, the same yesterday, to-day, and for ever."

All these rival principles have value if they be the outcome and offshoot of the Divine life, but by themselves they have failed. They are of the earth, of time, of sense, and belong to the world that is passing away; they belong to a lower sphere of life and activity; they cannot soar above the low level of self-created energy; they all fall short of "the excellency of the knowledge of Christ Jesus our Lord," short of the "light of the knowledge of the glory of God in the face of Jesus Christ;" far behind "the fulness of the blessing of the Christ."

I wish, then, to dwell for a few moments on that *blessing*, and then on the *fulness* of it.

The blessing of the Christ! what is it but a realization within yourself of that which is essential to Him—the benediction which comes from being *in* Christ, and having Christ in *you*, of being saturated with the thought and charged with the Word and filled with the Spirit of Christ? This blessing will be your *power* for good, your panacea for all evil, your energy and enthusiasm, your courage and joy in danger, your reason for every great enterprise and even for the smallest duty, your patience in disappointment, your endurance unto the end, your watchword at the gate of death, your welcome into the Father's house. Is it possible to overstate "the blessing of the Christ"? Doubtless it has many aspects. Every phase of the blessing, like the separate colours of the spectrum, is of immeasurable value; but to know how transcendent this blessing is, it may be well to glance at some of these aspects.

Thus (1) He is the ideal of your manhood. He is your greatest man. He surpasses in moral sublimity, and in the blending of many and often opposed qualities, all that we ever have heard or conceived of humanity at its very best. Combine the excellences of the highest men, who all suffer from some drawback, deficiency, or fault; let Moses and Confucius, Solomon and Socrates, St. Paul and Buddha, Augustine and Fenélon, Luther and Mohammed pass in review before Him, and their lustre pales and vanishes in the light of the Sun of Righteousness. You have a goal of perfection in His character which no evolution will ever transcend or equal. It will be a perpetual inspiration to you; and whether you are confronting the ideals of Greek and Barbarian, of Oriental sage, or European philosopher, He will always be far beyond and above them, and yet, within certain specific exceptions, He will be more available as an example, more imitable as a leader and master, than they all. We have become almost too familiar with the memorials of our Lord's character. We pastors and teachers at home almost covet the grand chance you have of making known such a manhood, such a miracle of majesty and mercy, of authority and sympathy, of spotless rectitude and passionate pity, of a purity and righteousness that brings men to their knees, and of a love which induces them in self-despair to kiss His feet, and cry with adoring gratitude, "Lord, I will follow Thee whithersoever Thou goest."

But (2) the blessing of the Christ is much more than this. Though He is the highest holiest Man, He is the only sufficient manifestation of the living God. His knowledge of God goes back into the past eternity. For ever and ever He has received and responded to an Infinite Love. You feel that, in having Him, you have taken hold of the central power and authority of the universe. In knowing Him, you know the Father. In that He is incarnate God, you can be calm amid the boundless spaces and the measureless time. The vastness of the universe does not bewilder you, the eternities do not crush your thought, the resistless powers do not abolish or mock you, for you know you have reached their very centre, and are at peace. When you cry "My Lord and my God," you know that this Lord has all power, and is able to save you, to shield you from the strange and awful possibilities of the unseen world. You are "persuaded that neither life nor death, neither angels, principalities, nor powers, neither things present nor things to come, neither height, nor depth, nor any other creature, shall be able to separate us from the love of God, which is in Christ Jesus our Lord."

(3) The blessing of Christ is not limited by the perfect Humanity and the absolute Divinity that are indissolubly blended in His person. The heart of man is broken, and needs a healer. The sins of your own life convince you that you would have cut yourself off from these consolations, unless you had found a Redeemer, an Expiation for sin, a Fountain which can positively take away and cleanse from all iniquity. The unsurpassable splendour of the Divine Humanity would be a dubious consolation after all, if you did not know that His infinite power brings all the perfections of God to bear on human sinfulness, to eat out the curse in our nature, to rectify our personal relations with the eternal order. The example and glory of Christ are not the *whole* of the blessing in which you live and move and have your being. The men and women whom you now are undertaking to teach have to face death, and to triumph over their fears touching a deeper and a second death. You have a sublime gospel to tell them: it is, that the Incarnate God bore their sins and carried their sorrows, that He represented on the Cross the sublime fact that the Lamb was slain from the foundation

of the world, and that, by His resurrection and ascension, He opened the eyes of those who knew Him best to see Him as the "Lamb slain in the midst of the throne." You have a gospel larger than the entire encyclopædia of science or civilization, when you declare without shrinking that the blood of Christ not only was shed for the remission of sin, but that it cleanseth from all unrighteousness. You have to show, by a perpetual effort, by endless illustration, by copious experience, by untiring zeal, by reiteration that should flow like waves upon the river of life, that this *pardon* does *cleanse*, that the cleansing by the blood of Christ is the sure and only guarantee of pardon. Men must hate and trample upon the sins which need such means to pardon them. The new life is the best assurance of faith. Holiness is the sacred and satisfying proof of the faith which has taken hold of God.

But again (4), the blessing or the benediction of Christ did not terminate on the cross or in the cloud which received Him from human sight. Strange flashes of light have gleamed from that unmeasured glory. The breath of Heaven —now gentle as a zephyr, soft as the waving of a dove's wing, exhilarating human hope, producing the mind of Christ in human hearts, leading the Church into every kind of truth, substituting the glory of Christ for the claims of self,—the Spirit of the Father and the Son—becomes the atmosphere breathed by the new-born soul. But this Heavenly breath is sometimes rushing and mighty, strong as tempest, compelling submission, subduing the earth, convincing the world of sin, of righteousness, and judgment to come.

Moreover, this sublime benediction has so wrought into the very warp and woof of human nature as to be inseparable from it ; nothing but absolute annihilation of the soul can destroy it: and thus, however perplexing and mysterious life before or after death may prove, untold myriads know that they are living in Christ and He in them, by the eternal Spirit that He has breathed into them. They have become conscious possessors of an eternal life, which sets all chance or change at defiance. This Christ-life within a man transforms him so radically that the difference between the new and the old life is more surprising than that which separates animal from human life, and it even approximates that which separates a corpse from a living man.

Now, every portion of this "blessing of the Christ" quivers and vibrates with the eternal force which constitutes the very being of every other portion. Every fraction of the reality has the tendency which may bring all spiritual things to bear upon the soul, just as the fractions of a magnet retain the magnetic properties and relations of the whole, and can be shown to stand in veritable and startling harmony with the poles of this great world. Wheresover you see the trembling of a soul in prayer and find the strange rapture of a sense of pardon, which has overcome the sense of sin, you know that the pulses of the Divine life have begun to beat, and that they will throb for ever in that soul.

But, once more, the most comprehensive blessing of all is, that Jesus is "Lord of all," is Master of every soul, Head of every community, King of every nation, the Supreme Son of God. They, to whom you can teach this, overcome the world, they triumph over the world's fashions, they are indifferent to the world's praise or blame, they outlive the world's smile, and, in the darkest hour, they cry, "Thine is the kingdom, the power, and the glory for ever!"

Now, in few words let me impress upon you that you are to enter upon your work in "the *fulness* of the blessing of the Christ." Half the evils which have afflicted the Church or arrested the Divine life have arisen from the dismemberment of the Christ; from losing sight of, or losing touch with, some essential element in this ample, this opulent blessing.

Some men are ready to ignore His Divinity, some as perilously to forget His human sympathy. Some generations have so exalted His character and example as to lose all appreciation of His priesthood and sacrifice, and the offering of His body once for all. Some have so emphasized His atonement as to lose sight of His regal claims, His awful righteousness, His commandments, and His Spirit. Many have so dwelt on the life He lived eighteen hundred years ago, as to conceal from view the fact that in Divine humanity He fills all things and lives for evermore, "the *same* yesterday, to-day, for ever." Go to your work in the *fulness* of the blessing of the Christ; comprehend with all saints the height and depth, the length and breadth, and know the love of Christ which passeth knowledge, that you may be filled with the fulness of Him that filleth all in all. May it produce the simplicity of life, the reverence and holy trust, the self-sacrifice and devotion, the prayerfulness and consecration, which a blessing so many-sided and abundant is designed to produce! Charge yourself anew with this fulness. Be in it, and let it abide in you, and you will not only communicate the great benediction to others, but will actually augment its force and vindicate its glory.

WAITING UPON THE LORD.

WAITING UPON THE LORD.

"They that wait upon the Lord shall renew their strength; they shall mount up with wings as eagles; they shall run, and not be weary; they shall walk, and not faint."—ISA. xl. 31.

THE problem of life becomes more weird as the ages roll. When self-consciousness is half awake, and the infant spirit is dancing like a feather in the breezes of spring, the thought of whence it came and whither it is bound does not haunt the memory or blight the future. When once the consciousness of self is stirred, and man finds that he is not what he seems, that the centre of his personality is behind all the veil of sense, that he *is* a spirit, that he *has* a body, then the conflict has begun which never ceases. The whole of life is a fruitless effort to crush or deny, to educate or soothe, the strange perturbation that has arisen. Doubtless Oriental mind, by hard schooling and hereditary habit, has to some extent applied a narcotic to the restless inquiry, and found solace in the belief of an all-encompassing illusion; and so it murmurs in words like these—

> "For all that laugh, and all that weep,
> And all that breathe are one;
> Slight ripple on the boundless deep
> That moves, and all is gone."

But, then, as Tennyson's ancient sage replies—

> "That one ripple on the boundless deep
> Feels that the deep is boundless, and itself
> For ever changing form, but evermore
> One with the boundless motion of the deep."

Neither asceticism, nor the forcible extinction of desire, nor the wildest license of illusive pleasure, nor intellectual denial of the soul, nor harsh blasphemy against nature or God, nor any struggling with the thews of a Titan to be free, nor any courage of despair, nor any contemplated suicide, ever really ended the strife. He who has found out that he *is* a spirit, akin to the tremendous Spirit that is back of all things, even of the tiniest and the vastest, must continue the search for some solution of his questions, "Whence came I?" "What and why am I?" "Whither am I bound?" These questions, now with rattling incisiveness, again with long low moan as of a wintry sea, are evermore heard within him.

Every life is confronted with the sharp cries that love hears issuing from the bewildering self-consciousness of another, and the multitudinous sighs of man become, as they are pondered, loud as mighty thunderings, and the tears that are shed over these mysteries would fill all the four oceans of the world.

Bereavement, loss of friendship, violent uprooting of old and quiet resting-places, perpetual apprehension and fear of what is worse, aggravate the sense of helplessness and dependence, and sometimes suggest, in the very extremity of despair, a gleam of hope.

The sense of collision with the Power which is above and behind all, the miserable aversion to what is best and wisest in it, enmity to the eternal Righteousness, goodness, and power, forbid rest and sap strength. Whensoever a man finds out that his inner self, his own spirit, is on one side and the Infinite force on the other, he may become alive to the fact that he is himself to blame for this enmity, that he is the cause of his own unrest; and the problem becomes even more intolerable. "Deep calleth unto deep."

Moreover, the consciousness not only of evil done but of duty left undone, of opportunities wasted, of "chains of lead about the flight of fire," of goals lost sight of, ends unfulfilled, and all the threads of life tangled and ravelled, begets further agony; and so we hear outside of us and within us booming up the cry, "Oh, wretched man that I am, who will, who can deliver me?"

Yes, verily! one can only look at the fierce haste after pleasure, the absorbing pursuit of gain, the loathsome struggle for pre-eminence under the mask of principle and patriotism and zeal for truth, as another form of the same despairing cry, "Who will show us any good?" Is it romantic, illusory in itself, to go to Isaiah of Jerusalem for some solace, some secret of peace? How can the Hebrew seer lift the burden off the heart of the Western world in the nineteenth century of Christendom? Yet, verily, when some of God's dear prophets have spoken their noblest and best, we find that the tones of their voice have set other prophetic souls vibrating with the same note, affirming the truth, confirming the utterance.

Some chords well struck waken resonant murmurs in all the corresponding strings of the great harp of human life. If we listen to Isaiah's triumphant discovery, we find it is enriched and deepened and made sonorous in many a word of Him who is the Word incarnate. "Wait upon the

Lord" finds its answer in "Come unto Me, and I will give you rest."

It is well-nigh impossible to unwind the meanings of this wondrous phrase. There are not fewer than twenty different words in the Hebrew and Greek Scriptures which are all translated by one English word "wait," and this simple fact shows us how the prophetic and troubled souls of God-taught men have strained and writhed to express the thought that was in them. I think they may be reduced to three fundamental ideas—*silence, hope,* and *eager expectancy*. The prophets call on their souls to *wait silently and patiently*, to *wait hopefully*, and to *wait expectantly*, for the Lord.

A few remarks on each of these notes in the great chord. Each note represents one element of relief, one attempt at the solution of the portentous questions which the soul awakened to know itself and to see its peril must ask with ever-deepening solemnity.

1. *Silence before God the Lord.* "Be still and know that I am God." "Truly my soul is silenced before God." When the Lord answered Job out of the whirlwind, Job answered and said, "I lay my hand upon my mouth. Once have I spoken and I will not answer, yea twice, but I will proceed no further." This silent waiting is the patient and still endurance, the quiet abiding in Christ our Jehovah. This is the patience which does not give way in the hour of trial which comes to try all those that dwell on the earth. This is the grace which has made the martyrs calm when the heaven did not open and send down avengers to save them from the lions or the hungry fire. To understand it at its loftiest and best we must go to Gethsemane and hear the Holiest One cry, "Not as I will, but as Thou wilt." This

is the secret of the noblest mystics who lost their self-will, not by obliterating consciousness, but by a sense of the holiness and goodness of the Lord God, so that they could lie content, absolutely silent, profoundly quiet and passive, in the arms of the besetting God. When we can thoroughly trust in the living God the mystery is read, the deepest shadow is accepted, the horror of great darkness is felt to be the hollow of the hand of Him who dwelleth in the thick clouds. This kind of waiting upon the Lord is closely akin to the abandonment of self which reconciliation with God insures at the beginning of our spiritual life, and is often much needed when new perplexities arise to our faith which the mere reason cannot solve and which no experience can adequately meet. There are moments of transition and unclothing, when the troubled and worried spirit had best be silent. Sometimes when the fancied ornaments of the temple of God are being removed by ruthless hands, we are tempted to think that the whole structure is about to fall and involve all that is most precious to us in immediate ruin. Let us wait silently and patiently, let us wait only upon Him, and we shall find that the removal of the supposed beauty adds to its true glory and its veritable stability. We may easily be induced by clamour and passion to suppose that some showy buttresses to God's truth and temple are essential to its continuance. Let us wait patiently, and we shall before long renew our strength of conviction in the imperishable solidity of the foundations which can never be destroyed. Those things which cannot be shaken remain, even when the earth and heavens are shaken and the elements are melting with fervent heat. Such silent waiting casts all the responsibility upon God, as upon One who is great enough and strong enough and wise enough to solve all problems in His own time and way. It does not hope, nor fear; it does not moan, neither does it sing. "In the Lord Himself," such silent watcher says, "I have confidence and strength." God is all and in all.

There are moments of fierce trial for old Christians, when certain formulæ seem to have vanished, some flowers and fruits of grace seem to be sucked out and squeezed of all sweetness, and some phraseology sanctified by long usage appears to have lost its savour and even its meaning. These discoveries are like looking into the burning fiery furnace, and the best form of our waiting upon the Lord is to be still, and know that God is God.

Moreover, there are physical trials and domestic losses quite beyond measurement and human endurance. The desolation is complete. The agony is piled up. The cross is sharp. The cruel disappointment can never be soothed. We who are finite are clashing swords with Infinite Power, and striking at and wounding ourselves on the thick bosses of Jehovah's buckler. Be still, my soul, and wait thou only upon the Lord. If thou knowest Him, thou perhaps wilt find, notwithstanding all thy fears, that—

> "His most holy name is Love,
> Truth of subliming import! with the which
> Who feeds and saturates his constant soul,
> He from his small particular orbit flies
> With blest outstarting! From himself he flies,
> Stands in the sun, and with no partial gaze
> Views all creation: and he loves it all
> And blesses it, and calls it very good!
> This is, indeed, to dwell with the Most High!
> Cherubs and rapture-trembling Seraphim
> Can press no nearer to the Almighty's Throne."

Such peace springs from the absolute submission and

perfect quiet of the soul. Thought dies into enjoyment. Desire is lost in ecstasy. Self-obliteration is complete. The mightiest Love has won the victory. The soul is loved sublimely, and entirely loves—whether in the body or out of the body, it knows not ;—

> "Rapt into still communion which transcends
> The imperfect offices of prayers and praise,
> The mind is a thanksgiving to the Power
> Which made it. It is blessedness and love."

Yet it must be admitted that quietism and stillness cannot cover the whole of our experience. Some thinkers make it the consummation of the religious life, and consider that to lose ourselves finally in God is the goal of all our striving, the heaven of all our faith. Such a treatment of it, however, savours more of the Oriental *nirvâna* than of the Christian life. Quietism closely approaches "absorption," *i.e.* if it be made an end rather than a means to an end. To reach it, the soul must cease to hope or fear, must school itself to become less even than the faintest ruffle on the bosom of the Infinite ocean of being, to be nothing, to lose even the power to know its own blissfulness. But if the stillness or silence be regarded as a means to an end, what is it but another name for full reconciliation with God? Perfect accord with the Divine majesty and mercy, such as is brought about by acquiescence in the Divine reconciliation with us through Jesus Christ our Lord, answers our yearning, but does not abolish our consciousness. God knows that there are many things whereunto He needs in His perfect wisdom and love to reconcile us. We become conscious of a damaged nature, and a rebellious heart and strange desires. Moreover, an unknown destiny haunts us. The wages of sin impend. We finish nothing, we achieve little, and our life is like a broken column and a smoking torch, and a cruel disappointment. He is Himself reconciled to us in the death of His Son, and He reconciles us to Himself under these strange conditions by the same mysterious awful fact. We appropriate the death of the second Adam, as we had previously realized as ours the sin and death of the first Adam. As in Adam all die, so in the dying of One for all, all died; and this death once realized is life and peace. We leave all then to God, and this is the earliest stage of the Divine reconciliation, and our souls are still. The little child can thus rest in the love of Jesus, the beginner in the Divine life knows the secret.

2. But this is not the whole idea of "waiting upon the Lord," for over the silently waiting spirit comes the breath of hope. It is reconciled, but it searches the meaning and end of its own reconciliation. The silence prepares to break forth into song. That human friendship is very deep indeed when twin souls are utterly quiet in one another's presence, when they can meet and part without a word, and yet the friendship grow and the love deepen. But such love as this always holds a future in its grasp. Sacred stillnesses inwardly yearn and hope for mutual expression. "Still communion" rises up into, and anticipates hopefully the ends of such fellowship. Because we are reconciled to God we find ourselves in the stress of a new contest. Hope is born in the breast of the weaned child. We see a goal to be pursued and an end to be secured beyond the simple fact of our reconciliation. We find ourselves in the midst of a plunging onward movement. What seemed like *stillness* is the equilibration of mighty forces, is the balance of the parts of our nature in their rushing race. The reconciliation reveals other forces and

adverse ones, principalities and powers which must be subdued under us, which are against us, but which we must more than conquer—nay, which we must transform into our allies. Being reconciled by the death of the Son of God, much more we are to be saved by His life. We are saved by cherishing a sacred desire. What we see, we do not hope for. But many things are invisible. We gaze still through a glass darkly; and we hope on and look upwards. So it comes to pass that much which Holy Scripture describes as waiting upon God, is a Divine longing. "My soul waiteth even in the depths, waiteth for the Lord more than they who watch for the morning." God gives us these desires after Himself. They are the prophecies of the fulness of His love. They are the veritable prayers of His elect who cry day and night unto Him. We have known something of resting in the Lord and waiting patiently and silently for Him, with wonder and with holy fear, but from this point we have gone forward, not backward, when we have proceeded to cry aloud unto God our strength, and to desire at least one thing, that we may not merely lie passive in His hands, but that we may see His fair beauty and drink of the river of His pleasure.

Nor (3) is this blending of silence and desire all that the saints of Holy Scripture have meant by "waiting upon the Lord." Another word is used by prophets which couples with desire an earnest EXPECTATION. To the simple idea of holy longing, St. Paul too binds another, viz. that of eager and strained anticipation. He sees the Christian athlete a-tiptoe, with an all but realized yearning for the crown, or bending forward with the eye on the goal, and the hand stretched forth to grasp the prize, not only with strong desire, but with full assurance of faith.

We may easily confound the higher and the lower, and invert the order of their excellency. Absolute quietude, a full reconciliation which desires nothing and hopes for nothing, and a satisfaction that does not even seek to respond to the Divine goodness, falls short of this full assurance. Verily, the beatific vision is more than a rest which scarcely knows that it sees, or is. The somnolences of some high-flown experience soon reveal the indolence of half-hearted reconciliation. Moreover, the heart that is being disciplined by the highest vision and the stoutest expectation is most alive to the work of God in the world of men.

Those who drink of the river of the Lord's pleasure, are already powerfully expecting this triumph over all that disfigures His kingdom. Noble work is done by those who know that God's love to the world cannot be a failure. Because they *see*, they toil. Because they expect great things *from* God, they do great things *for* God. Disappointment, dark clouds, angry storms of human hate; nakedness, peril, and sword, are powerless to crush those who are persuaded that nothing can separate them from the love of God. The despairing pessimism of our day is the child of agnosticism, is the cloud which rolls up from the "sunless gulfs of doubt." Those who wait upon the Lord are not dismayed by the past history, nor confounded by the present condition of the world. They are ever blending joy with sorrow. They "glory in tribulations also, knowing that tribulation works out patience, and patience experience, and experience hope, a hope which will not put them to shame because the love of God is shed abroad in their hearts by the Holy Ghost given to them."

It becomes, then, a comparatively easy task to understand how "they who wait upon the Lord," in these three senses "renew their strength."

(i.) *Silent* waiting upon the Lord, absolute resting in God and full reconciliation with the Father become a renewal of strength. Let us at the foot of the cross of Christ cast ourselves utterly upon God's strength, upon the imperishable foundations of His throne, upon His own sublimest characteristics, upon God Himself at His greatest and best, and we shall find that He confers even upon us the stability of His own Being, the sufficiency of His own righteousness. This is a process which may be reviewed, reconsidered, and done over and over again, so that we may prove, time after time, how strong is our resting-place. The Divine life is a continuous renewal of relations with God. The living plant, from the very beginning, continually puts on fresh forms, new shapes of beauty. From sun and air and earth, the life draws its sustenance. It rests, but renews itself day by day. So the most entire acquiescence and submission to the Divine will, produces continually a new form, a new flower, a new fruit of grace, till the purpose of the Father is fulfilled.

(ii.) The *hopeful* waiting upon the Lord shows that the new desires of the reconciled spirit correspond with the purposes of God. In other words, prayer is answered. These yearnings of the spiritual creation are a "renewal of strength." Their travailing in pain and their groanings over the bondage of the whole creation are not pessimistic nor despairing; they are Christ's own tears and travail in the members of which He is the Head, and thus they become vehement and sacred desires for the manifestation of the sons of God. "In this tabernacle we are burdened, earnestly desiring to be clothed upon with our house which is from heaven." Such counting on "the unseen and eternal," such looking for the glory of God, is a daily renewal of the "strength" to do this thing, and works out "the far more exceeding and eternal weight of glory."

In like manner (iii.) the *expectant* waiting, which pierces and lifts the veil of the future, verily triumphs over obstacles, works while it is day, and even at the midnight has its lamp burning and its loins girt for battle or for pilgrimage, or for entrance with the Bridegroom to the marriage festival of heaven and earth. This strong expectant waiting seems to offer a much higher conception of the consummation of our life than an eternal stillness does. The difference between our finite knowledge and the infinite fulness of reality in God suggests eternal progress—not the exhaustion and completion of effort, not the dead monotonous levels of even the loftiest character, but a perpetual *renewal of strength*.

The text suggests an apparent anti-climax in the imagery employed by the prophet. First, he spake of soaring like the eagle, then of coursing like the athlete, and, finally, of walking steadily along life's common way. Is this a climax or a bathos? I am inclined to think that Isaiah knew perfectly that the floating and soaring of the great eagle over the desert waste or mountain-top was, after all, though a lofty and blessed image of renewal of strength, not the highest. It represents a rapture, if you will; it is the image of one who can gaze undazzled on the sun. Yet the eagle cannot outsoar the atmosphere of earth by which it is sustained. Though it rises high, the chamoix and the chamoix hunter, too, may climb as far. The eagle soars, but with an eye on his prey. He hovers in almost awful stillness that he may drop plumb-down out of the azure to the quarry that his eye, unblenched by the unveiled sun, has the more keenly perceived. So it comes to pass that raptures of reconciliation and high upliftings of the soul do not always portend the fulness and completeness of joy, and the continuous renewal of strength. All through the history of the Divine life it is the same. Great is the power of patient, silent waiting for the slow "grinding of the mills of God." Wonderful is the peace which passes all understanding, when we can lift ourselves above the world, and scarcely sympathize with the sorrows of the race to which we belong, and are insensible to the stings and smarts and losses of this earthly life, having blown out the fires of anger and desire—yet the soaring on the wing of eagle or dove may not be the noblest victory. This was not the highest life of all. Isaiah himself had raptures, so had Balaam and Micaiah and Eliphaz. Some moments of sacred vision and hearing of unspeakable things were granted to Paul and John, and on the Mount of Transfiguration the Holy One was lifted up above the world of opposition into that of Divine love—yet that mountain height was not the goal of the life of Jesus. In every case the floating of the soul out into the empyrean of imagination and holy rapture were means to an end, *not* in itself the highest kind of life.

The *running of the race to a visible goal without weariness* may be a higher expression of the life that we ought to live. *Hopeful* waiting upon the Lord is more than a placid, patient, uninquisitive peace. The prophetic image suggests no rapturous escape from trouble, but a steady grasp of duty and pursuit of ends dear to God and man. It is the Old Testament anticipation of the apostolic summons: "Let us run the race that is set before us, looking to Jesus."

If we can run without weariness, more than human strength has been supplied to us. Hopefulness has stirred our peacefulness to higher consciousness. The waiting upon the Lord, which encourages us to rush onward along the paths and sorrows of life, in sympathy with men and with the end in view, seems more noble than rushing out of the world, and more akin with the life of Jesus, and with all the other ways of the Lord God Almighty. If we admit that the sons of Benedict and Dominic mounted on wings, the brethren of the Lord Jesus have renewed their strength with the hope and joy set before them, and so have endured the cross, despised the shame, and have set themselves down with Him upon His throne.

But, finally, must it not be freely conceded that the last clause of the prophetic image falls short of the first exhibition of the *renewal of strength?* It matters comparatively little whether it be correct or otherwise in rhetoric, yet for my part I cannot doubt that a steady onward plodding in a narrow path which winds and zigzags up a storm-cleft height; that a dutiful progress on a well-marked road, which, by monotonous levels, hides equally all the really distant past or future; that a march on—on—onwards, though the sky be dull, the fog around the soul, and no clear vision of the goal opening to the eye, accompanied nevertheless by an inward hopefulness and strong anticipation, is, if done without succumbing to the tremendous strain, in the poet-prophet's soul the *highest form of strength* drawn straight from the Lord God Himself. Of this, too, we feel assured that he who does outwardly press without discouragement along the pathway with an eager desire and expectation that Christ may be magnified in him, whether by life or death, may a little later in his pathway see the goal itself, and cry, "Henceforth there is laid up for me a crown of righteousness that fadeth not away." Such renewal of strength may do more for him still, for the time will come when St. Paul, having finished his course, having kept the faith, mounts on something stronger than an eagle's pinions. He veritably outsoars the atmosphere of earth. Eyes are given him strong enough to gaze without tears or fears on the unveiled face of the Father. He sees the regalia, the crown of righteousness, which the Lord, the Righteous Judge, will give to him, and not to him only, but also to all those who love His appearing.

CONSECRATION OF HEARTS AND THINGS.

Address preceding the celebration of the Holy Communion, at the opening of Mansfield College, Oxford, October 15, 1889.

CONSECRATION OF HEARTS AND THINGS.

The symbols of the broken body and shed blood of the incarnate Son of God always express for us our unutterable need and the fathomless depth of the righteousness and love of God. They have inexhaustible resources of suggestion. As the centuries move on with all their weight of mystery, of memory, and high endeavour, they mean more and more to us. Under their inspiration, men like ourselves have lifted up their hearts unto the Lord, and "with angels and archangels and all the company of heaven" have lauded and magnified the thrice holy Name. The sense of utter unworthiness has been rescued from undue dejection by the promise of a free pardon and the stirrings of a new and sacrificial life. The keen bliss of human love is sharpened by these memories of a love stronger than death. The shadows of the tomb are dissolved in the light ever gleaming from the Cross, or rather from the face of Him who was dead but is alive for evermore.

Enterprises of "great pith and moment" are only safely entered upon when, as at this service, we can realize the mighty presence of our Lord, and when we dare invoke that, which is the perpetual prayer and the constant beatitude of the Church. When our fathers in the wilderness finished their work a cloud covered the tent of the congregation, and the glory of the Lord filled the tabernacle, and whensoever, in the dead of night, amid the recesses of the catacombs, on the mountain sides, in the forests, in the dungeon or on the battlefield, the martyr-Church of many names has clasped by faith inseparable hands with all who loved the Lord Jesus Christ in sincerity, the cloud of glory has been seen and felt "a shadow by day and a fire by night, in the sight of all the Israel of God throughout their journeyings."

An enterprise of moment to the Church of Christ now reaches consummation. Numerous services of consecration have been solemnized on this site of many memories. Churches and colleges thus raised have embodied strong tendencies at work in the Church and State. Their significance to-day is proportioned to the strength of those ideas, to the loyalty and faithfulness of those who profess them, and to the intensity with which living men can realize in conjunction with them the Divine presence and approbation. In a similar manner, certain potent ideas and living principles of thought, of worship, and Divine service have been already crystallized into these walls. The buildings themselves are the creation of much personal enthusiasm, not only of worthy and learned men, but of poor saints, and they represent a dominant spiritual idea which may make another epoch in the history of the Church in England. With the memory of the dying love, with the fire of the living presence of our Lord, we hope to consecrate this place to Him and to His glory.

The dedication of the house to highest uses can only

be fully consummated by a conscious self-consecration to those uses. In the strength of a deep love to Him who alone confers on these principles and on these uses any value, let us grasp them with such fervour that they will become more to us than our own life, and dearer to us than we are either to ourselves or to one another. They will assuredly live and work in the higher life of England—of all the Churches of England—when we have all passed beyond the need of symbols, into the great reality where we shall see Him as He is.

Those are thrice blessed whose highest aims and whose practical services coincide. There is, however, one fear, one peril to be avoided in such cases; our lower motives, our proximate ends, have about them a certain overmastering force, a kind of brute strength; a species of mechanical energy and of rare glamour withal, which, even while they are bent in facilitating means of consummate value for effecting noble ends, condemn us often to rest satisfied with the proximate measures and to substitute means for the ends. May the highest ends be paramount to-day!

The immediate purpose which is obviously enshrined in these buildings, and which we seek to effect by them, is a higher training of the ministers of our free Churches. We desire in this institution to transcend that which has hitherto been achieved. We wish to give our young men a larger outlook into the world which they yearn to bless. Our passionate desire is that they may know the best things that are knowable; that they may apprehend, not only the needs and tendencies of their own clique or persuasion, but the conscientious convictions of men of other schools of thought; that they may drink deep draughts of knowledge; that they may sharpen with all available means their appetite for truth itself, by pursuing with enthusiasm some of the specialities of their great theme. We desire that they may learn the secrets of many minds, so as to unriddle the perplexities of some, and lift off the incubus which burdens the heart and conscience of others. We have so much confidence in the reality and glory of the Christian faith, that we have no fear of the result. Some who are suffering from that sensitiveness which Schleiermacher called "the phthisis of the intellect" may have to endure a furnace in which their strength will be sorely tried; but those who have veritably received the Divine life, who have entered consciously into the kingdom of God, who are born again of incorruptible seed by the Word of God which abideth for ever, will find the mission on which they are set and the message they have to deliver revealed to them anew in a veritable gleam of light. They will see more and more of the convergent forces which, with unresting progress, are unveiling the King of kings and bringing into view the destiny and redemption of the world by Jesus Christ. They will not lose in a superficial and exhausted mysticism their vision of One who is the Way, the Truth, and the Life of men.

Doubtless these are days of transition, when some positions once held most certain have been taken from us by the ever-continuous wear of the critical wave. Moreover, some modification of the way in which our fundamental truths are stated may be found imperative; but the Christian faith is stronger with every fresh conclusion of sanctified intelligence. There have been many such crises in the history of the Church and in the methods of Divine revelation, and God has not yet been driven from His own temple, nor is the Christ less manifestly real in His power and grace than He ever was. Consequently we accept without fear an inheritance and a possibility from which the sons of the Puritans were long debarred, and we hail an opportunity to bear more thoughtful witness than ever to that which is to us the primal truth of the bearing of the Incarnation of the Word upon the destiny of the human race.

These are a few of our practical aims and secondary motives. However numerous and noble they may be, they are simply the means in our hand to compass a sublimer end. What we aim at is something entirely beyond any machinery, any party triumph, any honour that we can achieve in doing what is in itself worthy or noble: it is nothing less than opening the kingdom of Heaven to all believers; it is the revelation of the Lord Christ to the world; it is the saving of those for whom Christ died; it is the proclamation of His gospel to the world.

The meaning of our communion service to-day is our fervent desire to bring the ultimate end of this special endeavour into the burning focus of the Divine Presence. We yearn to consume in this baptism of fire all unworthy, all insufficient motive. The altar is built, the sacrifice is laid on the wood, and the cry of our hearts is that the fire from heaven may descend. We know that one flash of light from the presence of the Lord will do more for the realization of the best wishes that are cherished to-day than could any conceivable addition to our resources, or any dazzling augmentation of our prestige.

God forbid that, as we take these symbols of an infinite sacrifice, we should be inwardly sighing for any end less than the glory of our Lord in the revelation of Himself to the world.

We know that advantages such as those which we here provide for our young ministers may be delusive; that mere culture of intellect, that richer and fuller education, like the oxen and sheep in the courts of the temple, like the tables of the money-changers, may be eminently convenient to a Sadducean priesthood, or attractive to a secularized Church, but may yet perpetrate a profanation in the view of the Lord of that temple. If our desire is only to gain pre-eminence or power by advanced culture, the Master will come with the scourge rather than with the approving smile, and His terrible voice will be heard, "Take these things hence."

We have a holy mission; we are the witnesses to a principle of consummate preciousness, the guardians of a truth concealed from many, the prophets of a mystery which has been hidden from many generations. If the fellowship of this mystery should pervade the Churches, then the consecration of these buildings will be an event and an epoch in the history of religious thought. Great movements have been favoured, persecuted, and finally triumphant in Oxford. Lollardy and Puritanism, enthusiasm for the past, strength of invincible intuitions, vehemence of drastic criticism, passions which first created and then burned the martyrs, have, in succession, swayed the minds of men. Here arose, too, that sense of the value of each soul of man, and the superb hope that a man alone with God might find his calling and election sure. Here the Evangelical Revival found for a time scope and impulse.

During the last fifty years a more notable movement took its origin in Oxford, one which has deeply affected all contemporary religious life. The past history of the

Church of England has been re-written, and a new conception of the Church as a whole has been fathered and fostered, which has exerted an incalculable force on millions. In this university there was obtained the vision of a vast catholic organization, which embraced in itself the whole past evolution of the Church, whether Eastern or Western, Anglican or Oriental, and this, notwithstanding irreconcilable differences between them.

It is true that these sections of the catholic Church have not been reciprocally conscious of their solidarity; yet, as far as Anglicans are concerned, learned and holy men have become pathetically alive to the existence of a Body visible to them within certain restricted lines of historic continuity and corresponding organizations. They have, by the power of sanctified imagination, seen the Divine life and the supernatural order in certain well-defined regions, and have cherished the hope, and cherish it still, that all Churches must at last blend into this sacred unity of the flock and fold of God. But is this the last word that can be spoken touching the unity of the spiritual body of Christ? May we not cherish, and in this very service of reverence and love express, our profound conviction that the great Evangelical movement of the last century, and the Anglo-Catholic movement of this century, are co-operating to produce a greater movement than either? It is not impossible that even we may have something to do in stimulating its progress and development. Should it once move forward on the wings of faith and love, it will prove the most potent and far-reaching of all the great upstirrings of mind and heart which have taken their origin in this university. Common interest in sacred learning, friendly intercourse, mutual observation, co-operation in common pursuits, will be its coadjutors; but the sublime motive power is nothing short of the indwelling of the Spirit of God in all sections of the Church. Then, by a new and irresistible impulse, they shall combine to fulfil the prayer of the Divine Lord, " that they all may be one, even as Thou, Father, art in Me and I in Thee, that they also may be one in Us."

If the unity between the Father and the Son be the test and the norm of the union of the Church for which the Saviour prayed, then the glory and the exceeding blessedness will not be realized in form of words, or in unanimous expression of thought. No consent to creeds or definitions, however accurate and comprehensive they may be, according to the wisdom of to-day, can answer the prayer of the Christ. No vast world-embracing ecclesiastical order can ever satisfy the conditions of the problem. The notion of a universal creed and of a universal monarchy of Christian ministries has been dispossessed of its pre-eminence by the inexorable logic of facts.

But in the mutual and common realization of the true body of Christ, wherever His Holy Spirit—the Spirit of the Father and of the Son—puts forth Divine life in the myriad-sided organism of the new humanity, it will fulfil the glorious prayer of the blessed Lord. This is no new phantasy. It is the oldest of all. The Divine life, the new spiritual Sonship to God, is a fact; and the cry from the regenerated soul, from the adopted child, "Abba, Father," indicates and creates a *real* brotherhood, not a mere society. The elect souls in every Church have for ages been discovering this blessed reality. *Ubi Christus ibi ecclesia* has been the sacred talisman by which many cruel controversies have been reconciled. Noble testimonies to the triumphant principle have been borne by men whose life has sweetened the very breath of the world. Our own peculiarity is that we are the special guardians of a principle which has seemed at times too ethereal to live as a prominent form of Church life. I know we are far from fully embodying it in our own life; but if we depart from it, we utterly fail in our distinct and specific mission. Nevertheless, when the hour comes that the vigorous representatives of what are called free Churches can see the kingdom of God in all its other manifestations, whether in Rome or Constantinople, Geneva or Canterbury, and when the most spiritual, devout, and conservative members of the historic Churches can recognize and act upon the recognition of the Divine life, of the brotherhood in Christ, of the supernatural order beyond the pale and boundary hitherto assigned; when the union between such as are one in Christ becomes a mutual indwelling such as that between the Father and the Son, then *all will be one* according to a higher ideal than has ever yet been powerfully embodied among men. The Anglo-Catholic conception is a wonderful step in the right direction. It avails to overleap the most formidable barriers of confession, discipline, and practice. It offers its sense of brotherhood, moreover, to those who do not reciprocate the sentiments, nor admit its orders, nor give back the kiss of peace; and it seems to us that the Church principle of which we are the guardians does but carry out to its full expression a similar law of love. I dare to hope that the tiny stream which bursts to-day from its long-hidden sources here, may contribute to swell that vast, bright, abounding river of life, by the banks of which the historic Churches will drink deep draughts, and which will most assuredly lave the walls of "the city built for the perfected spirits of the just."

This prophetic conception has been cheering the noblest spirits in all the Churches. Wherever life has been more than form, and the spiritual body more than its raiment, this glowing hope has burned on the altar. The sacred fire has been extinguished, and even its custodians have sometimes smothered it in their eagerness to add fuel to the flame; nevertheless, it is fast becoming a world-wide illumination. This enterprise of ours is but one involuntary expression of a vast force of sanctified judgment, without which our present action would have been impossible, and it bids fair to transcend the conception of Wicliff and of Cranmer, the burning breath of Wesley, the far-reaching ideal of Newman and Pusey, and will be, in fact, the supplement and the complement and eventually the realization and the co-operation of them all.

At present we have only a faint adumbration of what a full Pentecostal effusion of the Holy Spirit must achieve. The spiritual temple rises in the midst of much debate.

> "O God, Thy architecture meets with sin,
> For all Thy fame and fabric is within.
> There Thou art struggling with a peevish heart,
>   Which sometimes crosses Thee, Thou sometimes it;
> The fight is hard on either part;
>   Great God doth fight, He doth submit.
> All Solomon's sea of brass and world of stone
> Is not so dear to Thee as one good groan.
> And truly brass and stones are heavy things,
>   Tombs for the dead, not temples fit for Thee,
> But groans are quick and full of wings;
>   And all their motions upward be;
> And, ever as they mount, like larks they sing:
> The note is sad, yet music for a king."

"The earnest expectation of the creation waiteth for

the revelation of the sons of God." At present they are not fully revealed; not yet can they even see each other: but as the mutual glances are interchanged a new meaning will be given to sacraments and orders; a fresh set of facts will be supplied to agnostic historians and philosophers; the souls of the martyrs will live again; intolerance will die in the new atmosphere that circles round the earth; criticism, however eager, will forget to sneer, and the world will believe, as it has never yet done, in the presence of the Christ who liveth for ever and ever. When this flood of life overflows the ramparts which divide us, they will in these great waters be only rocky islets in a boundless sea.

Let us draw near, then, to the symbols of a perfect love; let us hail the signal that the living Christ who died for our sins is in the midst of us. The special glory that beams from the cross of our Lord Jesus Christ, on hearts broken by a sense of sin, shame, and peril, is so dazzling that such cannot fail to see when they turn thence—as turn they must, to daily duty and to absorbing affairs of the world and of the Church—the spectrum of that Christ still in their field of view. It is strange, but most blessed, to find that, instead of confusing their mental picture of other things, that spectrum harmonizes with and explains them all.

We turn with deepest reverence once more to Him the symbols of whose living and dying and resurrection are renewed and spread before us. We humbly seek to use them now as records of all the mighty history of the kingdom of God, as significant tokens of all that our Lord has done for us and would have us do, the absolution and remission of all our sins, and the gift of eternal life. We desire to lose ourselves once more in Him. Bought by His precious blood, we desire to blend our bitterest sorrow for sin, our uttermost shame at the sins of even our holiest service, with our eucharistic shout of adoring gratitude. We dare to believe that He has taken upon Himself the responsibility and task of our full redemption, and that He is able to accomplish it. We, being many, are one loaf, seeing that we are partakers of the one bread, and we enter afresh into the unity of the spiritual body of Christ. We are seated at a table where the apostles, prophets, martyrs, saints and confessors of every age are feasting still. We join with the Fathers of the Early Church, and with many who were cast out as evil thinkers and wrong-doers, with Reformers and Puritans, and with those who swore Holy League and Covenant in their blood, and we know we are one in Him. We are creating no new society, but realizing the fact of a brotherhood created by the Holy Ghost. We are not inaugurating but claiming a fellowship with all who love our Lord Jesus Christ in sincerity.

"MINISTERS THROUGH WHOM YE BELIEVED."

Address preceding the celebration of the Holy Communion, at Cheshunt College Chapel, at the formation of the Cheshunt Union of Former Students, January 16, 1888.

"MINISTERS THROUGH WHOM YE BELIEVED."

"What then is Apollos? and what is Paul? Ministers through whom ye believed; and each as the Lord gave to him."—1 COR. iii. 5.

THIS moment is unique in the history of the college. Many dates are red-lettered in its calendar. Hours of deep impression have come and gone. Of its father, the friend of its foundress, it may be said, as was sung of Dante,—

> "From land to land,
> Like flame within the naked hand,
> His body bore his burning heart."

Missionaries, scholars, preachers, pastors, quiet labourers for God's truth have caught some of their earliest inspirations from its sacred memories. In lonely places, in distant regions, its freemasonic token has been of service. A goodly number of brave workers for Christ have often been stirred to better service by realizing their Cheshunt brotherhood. Not a few of your comrades have joined the company of the perfect ones within the veil, and will not have altogether forgotten us. They are not far away from us to-night, when, for the first time in our history of a hundred and twenty years, a serious effort has been made to combine and exchange our manifold emotions, to give zest to present duties by renewing our early consecration. The vinculum that has held you together has been very elastic, apparently fine as a gossamer thread, and yet it has been strong enough —I hardly know how or why, save that the Lord has willed it—to draw you together and induce you to revisit Cheshunt as a sacred place. The special charm is, that you have not gathered to hear some famous preacher or illustrious chairman, nor to inaugurate a new constitution, nor to contest some principle that you have felt to be endangered; not for mutual admiration, nor for the honour and prestige of our college, but simply for the glory of God, out of love to one another, and faith in one another's power, by His grace to kindle a new enthusiasm and loyalty for Christ and His kingdom.

Some explanation may be found in this, that here was the "birthplace of deep love" and much sacred friendship, and if Cheshunt were not the cradle of your Divine life, yet it was the spot where that supernatural life touched maturity, where, after much questioning and many prayers, you began in a deep sense consciously to *be*, to enter on "the eternal now." Here many of you came into more intelligent communion with apostles and prophets, and so to climb "the altar-stairs," until you found deeper fellowship with the Father, and with His Son, Jesus Christ. Did you not here do battle with the seven deadly sins? Was not self-conceit smitten? Did not self-control and self-sacrifice take the place of wilful self-pleasing? Did not the healing of pardon and of discipline follow the assurance of faith? Perhaps here the one tremendous chance of life loomed for the first time like a vast comet on your midnight sky, and TRUTH, veiled but beautiful, invested with much drapery, but *living*—no mummied corpse of dead men's thoughts, but the veritable thought of the Eternal, perfect and peerless,—here dared you to look on her face and live. Here you began to understand the terms which you had used from earlier days. Many a religious phrase which had erewhile been only a blank cheque was consumed to ashes; but some of these blank cheques were signed by God, and countersigned by your own conscience, and were thenceforward transformed into boundless wealth.

Having once beholden the glory of God in the face of Jesus Christ, you begin to wonder at the *sang froid* with which otiose assent was readily given to the very same ideas which, when *you* discovered them, shook your whole being to its centre. Flattering dreams of being able to compel men to see and feel with you, led you on. Bitter disappointments were soothed by gracious illusions, and the sympathy of brothers beloved. In many a sacred corner of the college, coteries have solved the problems of the ages. The puzzles of metaphysics vanished. Theories of evil and of death, of atonement and life, the claims of Rome and Westminster, of Tübingen and Halle, have been settled out of hand, to say nothing of ecclesiastical affairs that were nearer home.

How we smile in after days, not cynically, but sweetly, on our sanguine hopes and the infallibilities of our boyhood! I do not wonder, then, that you should have anticipated some pleasure, perhaps not unmixed with pain, when asked to come and take a bath in the fountain of sunrise, to resume with manhood's strength some of the glances of the infancy of your higher intellectual and moral life, to gather round the cross of Christ, to cherish a new hopefulness, to become more conscious of your calling of God and your mission in the world, and to renew the testimony you have to give to spiritual reality, alike in theological thought, in Church principles, in Christian life, and in holy enterprise.

Many of you can gratefully record years of service. You have wielded pen and pencil and pilgrim staff. In the pulpit, on the platform, in the professor's chair, in the direction of great institutions, in the guidance of political opinion, in hand-to-hand encounter with idolatry, intemperance, poverty, and sin, you have been fulfilling your course; yet there is not one of us who does not with a sigh confess that the service he has rendered has fallen far below the ideal that once rose enchantingly before him. We all acknowledge the intrusion of selfish consideration, the close proximity of unhealthy dispositions and morbid desires. Much of our ministerial life has resembled the "green ear" of the parable, rather than the fruit which it promised but failed to realize.

The tares which confuse, the thorns which choke the heavenly life have not been wanting. For one, physical weakness or shattered strength; for another, cruel domestic sorrow has impeded work. Some have had to mourn over the rivalry of sects and the feverish vitality which pulses in all our organization; others have shrunk dispirited from the higher attractions which the world in many forms presses on those whom they most wish to influence. Some of us have had to suffer occasional paralysis from straitened resources, or from the awkwardness of temper, or the grumbling of our fellow-workers. Our excellent friends are often loud in their appreciation of some ideas suggested by a stranger, which we had been vainly striving to hammer into them by long courses of instruction.

Perhaps we have all at times felt awestruck with the problems which have perpetually come to the front, and have been more or less bewildered by the acute crises that have followed one another in the world of thought. We dare not deny that at times the solid earth has seemed to tremble under our feet. Even the kingdom of God, that cannot be shaken, has appeared, as we received it, to quiver and reel. In our present retrospect we may, however, remember that the tempest which breaks over each man's soul is often peculiar to himself; he it is who is being shaken, not God's truth. It must be confessed also that the rainbow which the unveiled sun paints upon the threatening but departing cloud is subjective. In this case we have been consoled by the direct radiance upon our own soul of the Sun of Righteousness. That Sun may have been hidden for a while, but has soon emerged from the interception whether of a hurrying satellite or a passing cloud.

The Church of God has been always in the purgatorial flame. But we may say of this, as Virgil said to Dante,—

> "Be well assured, that should'st thou here abide
> Within this womb of flame a thousand years,
> No loss of e'en one hair should thee betide."

The kingdom of our Lord and of truth is by its very nature militant, but invincible. It is tossed by tempest and upheaved by earthquake, beleaguered by the spirits of evil, and in constant peril from enemies and treacherous friends; but the gates of hell will not prevail against it. The Lord knows that in bidding us defend it, He has given to us a task impossible to our unaided strength. The adjustment of the claims and mutual relations of the Divine and human in nature, in revelation, in the person of the Christ, in the spiritual life, is a feat passing wonderful. In ourselves we have no strength equal to it. The Lord Jesus said, on the night of the Passion, to His chosen apostles, to Peter, Matthew, John, " Separated from Me, without *Me, i.e.* by the aid of your own wit or wisdom, by your own power or holiness, *you can do nothing.*" We, too, have found His words to be true; and only in the degree to which we have drawn upon His supernatural strength, felt His precious blood cleansing us from sin and coursing through the veins of our spiritual nature, and the Divine life of the God-Man thrilling through our whole consciousness, and transforming us into the members of the spiritual Body of which He is the Head, have we ever done any one thing of the smallest advantage to God or man. We are here, dear Lord and God, gathered to-night to eat Thy flesh and drink Thy blood, to assimilate Thy Divine-human nature, to live by Thee, "that our sinful bodies may be made clean by Thy body, and our souls washed in Thy most precious blood, that we may evermore dwell in Thee and Thou in us."

Let us encourage one another, comfort one another, with the words of life, and open our hearts to receive a new baptism of the Holy Ghost, so that we may be able to see God, to discern the Divine working, as we resume the duties to which in various ways He has called us. In every case, and notwithstanding our disappointments, the work done has been immeasurably more than an illusive dream. The result of it has been more sacred, more blessed, more spiritual in its issues, than in our most sanguine youthful hours we prayed that it might prove. Once we aimed at the production of a glorious *leafage* which should add to the strength of our individual life, the honour and admiration of men. Now we are satisfied with nothing but *fruit*, which, though it exhausts our strength, is the veritable end of our existence. Once we loved our life, and lost it; now we have hated our life, and learned to find it only in Him.

I feel, more than I can possibly express, the honour and happiness of greeting so many of you, who have been my joy and crown of rejoicing, and the solemnity and sacredness of the opportunity of once more addressing you.

What is the one supreme and sublime end of our calling—either as workers in the Church, as preachers of the gospel, as teachers of the young, as heads or leaders of colleges or societies or unions of Churches, or as missionaries to heathen nations? May I not put the question in St. Paul's burning query, "What then is Paul? What is Apollos?" Is Paul the man who has been thundered to from the skies, or caught up into heaven to hear unspeakable words? Does he glory in his wisdom, or his might, or his gifts? Are these the essential features of the apostolate? Nay, verily! What is Apollos? Is he the Alexandrine philosopher? the eloquent writer? the ingenious rhetorician? These characteristics utterly vanish in comparison with the essential purpose and prime factor of his call. What is Paul, what Apollos, but *ministers through whom ye believed?* The entire end of their existence in the world was to create faith in others. The apostolate was a means to an end; the end was the faith of the Church. The faith of a little child, of some slave of Chloe, of some son of Stephanas, was more precious to God than the entire career of an apostle *per se*. So our pastorates, our publications, our Churches, our colleges, our great societies, our sacraments, have one sublime end in view, immeasurably greater than themselves. All these are but a ministry by which men believe; God honours the means, He loves the end.

Is it necessary to justify this statement?

Perhaps it might be necessary in the outside world of men, or when face to face—as we may be to-morrow—with the titanic energy of modern unbelief, or when confronted with the cynical scorn of those who cry, "Let us know what you can do. Let us see what you are. Let us have proof of your character. We care nothing about your faith." It may be indispensable to vindicate the apostle when in the presence of those who minimize the force, discount the advantage, and empty out the contents of faith; but, even here and now, it is not without some advantage to inquire, What do we mean by producing faith? and how are we continuously to pursue this apostolic function?

I would not exaggerate the significance of faith, nor put into it what is not of its essence; I would not define faith by its own consequences, and then deduce those consequences from faith. That mistake would be equivalent to the fault charged by Dr. Martineau on the physicists, —who first imagine an atom and a unit of force; who, secondly, mentally transfer to the atom thus conceived, all the potencies and glories of nature; and then, thirdly, by an apparently logical process, deduce these from the primordial atom.

If by faith I choose to connote all the mystery of the Divine life, all the beauty of Christian character, all the fruits of holy living, it would be an apparently easy task to show how they, one by one, burst from their germ and follow from their source. We cannot, any of us, produce faith in this comprehensive sense; we cannot bring about moral surrender to God; we cannot recreate the soul of man. The living God, by His Holy Spirit, can alone regenerate, can alone produce the heavenly mind, or give eternal life. There is, however, a work for us to do. Our mission is to help men to perceive the substance, the underlying reality of all we hope for, to make evident the things unseen.

Even Nature here may help us. The underlying substance is indefinitely more than the accidents by which we are enabled to recognize it. The all-pervading force is unspeakably more than all the manifestations of it. This substance, this force, is more than nature; it is the supernatural. Our *ego* is again unutterably more than all the states and impressions with which some would confound it. It is above nature, intimately related with Cause itself. All cognition of the substance of all things is the result of the faith-principle of our inmost *ego*. We cannot repudiate it without mental suicide. This same faith-principle takes hold of the eternal reality that has been manifested to our understanding. It is by means of it that we see the invisible, mount up on wings from the temporal to the eternal, and find the awful Holy One with whom, verily, we have to do, whether we like it or not. As soon as the object of faith takes shape, we find ourselves confronted with abundant hostility from the flesh, from the principalities, powers, rulers of the darkness of the world, who strive with passionate eagerness to close every chink through which the light of eternity, the revelations of a living God, may gleam. There are those who sedulously toil to transform every hint of the supernature above, around, and within us, into the closed circle of nature. Miracle, inspiration, incarnation, atonement, spiritual life, sacrificial consecration, eternal blessedness, are all reduced to fleeting phenomena, of that which is called nature. However comprehensive nature may thus become, and though we identify all her ways with the purposes and order of the Eternal, yet He is infinitely more than they. We are summoned, it seems to me, to lead men to feel, to see, to handle the unseen and eternal, to lift them up into the Holiest of all, and bid them look and live.

Let us take the sublime fact which we commemorate this evening, namely, the Sacrifice of the Incarnate Word for our sins, the Body broken, the Blood shed for us, and shed for the remission of our sins. If by faith we press behind these memorials, behind these accidents, behind all the words by which we speak of it, to the substance,—if we grasp the unseen and eternal thing here foreshadowed,—we come into direct contact with an almost blinding light. The glory of God in the face of the dying Christ is so unutterably resplendent, that only the eye of faith can bear it; but if it be indeed the glory of God, then it is the outflashing upon us of that which is eternal, which was before all worlds, is now, and for ever. Infinite love and absolute righteousness, exhaustless pity and consummate sacrifice, the inflexibility of eternal law accepting the anomaly of humiliation and pain, the glorification of death in the agony of holy love, God, at His very best, and as He is from eternity to eternity, breaks on our vision! The Lamb of God slain from before the foundation of the world, the Lamb in the midst of the throne, stands before our inward eye. Our faith lays hold of these when we see Jesus. These outstretched bleeding hands, as we look on them by faith, become the everlasting arms, "mighty to save." It is this faith in the unseen and eternal that it is our function to evoke, by all our ministries of whatever kind. Only so far as we call it out, can we fulfil our course. Such a mission is worth living for, worth dying for.

Some of us have occasionally been shy of this conception of the eternal God; but what tremendous power there is in the truth of the Divine Nature, just as it is. Sacrificial but eternal love to His creature blended with burning wrath against sin. All His dispensations in the past, all the temporal mission of the Son and of the Spirit are expressions of His eternal nature, revelations not only of what He once was or did or said, or of something that He may perchance be or do in some unknown future; but of what He is at this present hour, and will be for ever (Ps. xc.). Let us ponder for a moment our infinite need of it. Surely nothing can exceed the pathos and the misery of our condition, whatever science or philosophy may say to comfort us. Child and woman, sage and peasant, rich and poor, king and prophet, poet and practical philanthropist, have felt the insupportable burden of existence when once the portentous fact of sin has been perceived. Many religious teachers have sought to solve the problem. Some have emphasized the pain, and have sought, like Buddha, refuge in *nirvâna*. Others have dwelt on the omnipotence of God, and sought, like Mahomet, to make all things straight by a *tour de force*. Some have lowered the sense of right to the level of etiquette, and have, like Confucius, lost the sense of futurity. Others, under the power of Hindu philosophy and ritual, have so reduced the consciousness of individuality, that man has appeared to be but a wave lifted upon a boundless ocean, drifted for a period—which is like the twinkling of an eye—from nowhere to nowhere. Many in these days would have us renounce our inquiry and lose our transcendental fears in the admiration and *cultus* of humanity, and they tell us that the future evolution of our race will settle all the inequalities and wipe out the old scores; while others assert that poetry will take the place of religion, and will prove strong enough as an anodyne for our irresistible conviction of enmity against God, endeavouring thus to throw so much charm around " the service of man," as to make the coming age indifferent to " the service of God " !

Now, our hopefulness consists in this, that the genuine Christian experience is such a contact with the living God in all the grandeur and fulness of His Being, that it offers the one solution at which all other forms of pseudo-religious experience aim, but never find. By faith in the Christ of God we have learned to blend in one indivisible act the most poignant sense of sin, the most vivid imagination of evil, with the perfect assurance of pardon; to cherish at one and the same time the uttermost sense of impotence and insignificance with the overpowering conviction of conscious union with the Eternal One. We learn with the pang of a broken spirit to shout "Hosanna;" to be veritably crucified and buried with Christ, and nevertheless to live; to transform the cup of blood into a cup of thanksgiving.

The brotherhood of man is the indefeasible concomitant of the righteous Fatherhood of God, as revealed in the cross of Christ. Every movement of love to man, every device of Christian heroism, every act of consecration to Christ, every effort to take upon ourselves some of the sin or sorrow of another, opens to us the heart of Christ, which is the lens whereby we can gaze upon the Lord God Himself in the eternity of His blended beauty, the awfulness of His holiness, the fathomless ocean of His boundless love. How infinitesimal the distinction of sect, of society, of office, of method, when we are set upon securing the great end—namely, so speaking, acting, living, loving, that men may believe and live.

What we have to do is to produce *faith*—in the unseen and eternal; God Himself will do all the rest.

But how? *First* of all, it is obvious, by exercising it. We must ourselves believe and live. The blind cannot lead the blind, nor set the telescope for vague and wandering eyes. We often deceive ourselves by the illusion that we can induce a deeper faith than we feel. We try, it may be, to lift people to our own shoulders, and then almost in despair to exclaim, "Now *you* may see what I cannot;" but little comes of it. There is much constant communion with invisible things demanded from every man who would induce faith. Incessant prayer and waiting upon God are needed by us all. We should, I think, sometimes make inroads upon our abounding tasks, clear a space of time, and refresh and recreate ourselves herein with meditative vision and abandonment to Christ. The greatest realities of our life lie behind that of appearance. The kingdom of God is within us. By inward waiting upon God we renew our strength, we mount up with wings, we see the invisible, we run the race, we endure to the end.

Secondly, we must cherish the consuming desire to produce faith. I know that I have the desire, but I sometimes fear that it is only the desire to have the desire, and sometimes, alas! the credit of the desire. The desire often becomes languid, and I am tempted to feel that perhaps something else may be as good for me as that faith which is the evidence of things unseen. Can we stir up one another to desire the thing itself, to desire to win souls, to *be* "ministers by whom men believe"?

Thirdly, I feel convinced that we should aim at the production of *faith*, rather than aim, as we sometimes exclusively do, at the production of the fruits or consequences of faith. The kingdom of God is as if a man sows seed in his field; he sleeps and rises, night and day, and the earth brings forth of itself. The husbandman does not plant germs without roots, or thread either real or artificial flowers upon barren stocks. How much, then, belongs to God in all this work? And yet Almighty God seems to crave the aid and call for the service of human hearts and hands in the great work of creating faith in the minds of His children.

"Do ye now believe," said the dying Christ, with almost plaintive tenderness, "that I came forth from God?"

Then, when He had the assurance that they did believe, and even though He knew that *one* would betray Him, and that they *all* would forsake Him, He seemed to say, "Now I can go onward to the cross." Humanly speaking, if they had not believed, the Church of God would have perished that night in its cradle of sorrow and blood. All periods of revivals have been times of vision. The victory that has overcome the world has been faith in the Son of God. Times of retrogression and horrors of deep darkness have passed over the Church, but only when faith has been weakened or exhausted, paralyzed by superstition, or encumbered by incomprehensible propositions, or, it may be, counteracted by the feverish and deadly excitement of the visible, the sensual, and the selfish. Some knowledge is indispensable to faith, but faith is necessary to the knowledge which is eternal life. Some of this knowledge is indispensable to love; but "he that loveth not, knoweth not God, for God is love."

Fourthly, we cannot instrumentally excite faith in others without deep sympathy with them. We must understand their difficulties, and admit that some of their perplexities are genuine and honest, are the product of neither their conceit, their waywardness, nor their depravity. There is honest doubt on the part of those who are anxious to believe, but cannot. There is an agnosticism which prepares the way for faith. But let us not forget that there have been times and Churches in which for a while the chief apparent function and desire of the priest or presbyter has been to scatter confidence, undermine belief, and dissolve faith. God save you from this deadly fashion. It is well at times to rush forth into the open plain that we may see the stars of God. We must understand the temptations of men if we are to indicate firmly the way of escape, or bring before them the counter-attraction of the Cross. How difficult it is to get so close to a brother as to inspire an admiration for that which he slights, or scorns, or fears, or loathes. You cannot force a man to feel with you about really good music, poetry, painting, or argument, if his prepossessions are all the other way. You will not succeed by simply abusing his ignorance or scoffing at his lack of perception. You must take him hand in hand, and lead him out of his bad taste, and put the true beauty before him until his taste flows into harmony with your own. So we should strive to set forth the Christ in such beauty and power that we shall obtain the answering fulness of admiring and adoring contemplation. Only by much study, by purged vision, by prolonged training, by earnest prayer, by manly effort, can we undertake the solemn function of leading men to enter into the faith and fellowship of the Son of God.

BIBLIOGRAPHY.

Beginnings of the Divine Life. 1858. Third Edition, 1860. Six Sermons. Elliot Stock.

Notes of the Christian Life. A Selection of Sermons. Macmillan. 1865.

John the Baptist, being a contribution to Christian Evidences. Congregational Union Lecture. 1874. Second Edition, 1876. Hodder and Stoughton. Third Edition, with new Preface, 1890. Congregational Union of England and Wales.

Joint Author of *Yes and No, or Glimpses of the Great Conflict.* Three volumes. Macmillan and Co. 1860.

Joint Author of *Commentary on the Prophecies of Hosea and Amos* in Bishop Ellicott's "Old Testament Commentary for English Readers." 1884. Cassell and Co.

Editor of *Ecclesia.* Church Problems considered in a Series of Essays. 1870. Second Edition, 1871. (Contributed Essay on *The Forgiveness and Absolution of Sins.*) Hodder and Stoughton.

Editor of *Ecclesia.* Second Series, 1871. Contributed Essay on *The Holy Catholic Church.* Hodder and Stoughton.

Author of *Commentary on the Pastoral Epistles.* Published in First Series of *The Expositor.* Hodder and Stoughton.

The Philosophy of Prayer, and other Essays. 1882. Religious Tract Society.

Buddhism and Christianity, a Comparison and Contrast. "Present Day Tract Series." Religious Tract Society.

Athanasius: His Life and Life-Work. Church History Series, 1889. Religious Tract Society.

Introduction to the Gospel of St. John, with Exposition and Commentary. "Pulpit Commentary." Two volumes. Third Edition, 1891. Kegan Paul, Trench, and Co.

Editor with Rev. Dr. Allon of *British Quarterly Review*, 1866–1874. Articles—*Philosophy and Religion of August Comte; Our New Religions; Religious Systems, Ancient and Modern; Montalembert's "Monks of the West;" The History of the Doctrine of the Atonement; The Buddhist Pilgrims; Congregational Ministry and its Education; Religious Ideas and Modern Thought; The Life of August Comte;* etc., etc.

Contributor to Drs. Smith and Wace's "Dictionary of Christian Biography." Articles on *Eusebius of Nicomedia; Eusebius of Samosata; Fulgentius of Ruspe; Fulgentius Ferrandus; Frumentius; Gregorius of Neocæsarea; The Ethiopian Church; The Sabæans;* etc., etc.

Preachers of the Age.

In uniform crown 8vo. Volumes, with Photogravure Portraits reproduced, in most cases, from unpublished Photographs. Cloth extra, price 3s. 6d. each.

I. LIVING THEOLOGY. By His Grace THE ARCHBISHOP OF CANTERBURY.

II. THE CONQUERING CHRIST, and other Sermons. By the Rev. ALEXANDER MACLAREN, D.D., of Manchester.

III. VERBUM CRUCIS. By the LORD BISHOP OF DERRY.

IV. ETHICAL CHRISTIANITY. By the Rev. HUGH PRICE HUGHES, M.A., of the West End Wesleyan Mission.

V. THE KNOWLEDGE OF GOD, and other Sermons. By the LORD BISHOP OF WAKEFIELD.

VI. LIGHT AND PEACE, and other Sermons. By the Rev. HENRY ROBERT REYNOLDS, D.D., President of Cheshunt College.

VII. FAITH AND DUTY, and other Sermons. By the Rev. A. M. FAIRBAIRN, D.D., Principal of Mansfield College, Oxford.

VIII. THE JOURNEY OF LIFE. By the Rev. CANON W. J. KNOX LITTLE, of Worcester.

IX. PLAIN WORDS ON GREAT THEMES. By the Rev. J. OSWALD DYKES, D.D., Principal of the English Presbyterian College, London.

X. SERMONS. By the LORD BISHOP OF RIPON.

XI. MESSAGES TO THE MULTITUDE. By the Rev. C. H. SPURGEON, Pastor of the Metropolitan Tabernacle.

XII. AGONIÆ CHRISTI. By the Very Rev. WILLIAM LEFROY, D.D., Dean of Norwich.

Volumes will follow in quick succession by other equally well-known men.

LONDON: SAMPSON LOW, MARSTON & COMPANY, LIMITED, St. Dunstan's House, FETTER LANE, FLEET STREET, E.C.